HELLROARING

Fifty Years on The Big Mountain

JEAN ARTHUR

WHITEFISH EDITIONS • WHITEFISH, MONTANA

Whitefish Editions
Whitefish, Montana
First edition published 1996
Copyright © Jean Arthur, 1996
All rights reserved under International and Pan-American Copyright Conventions. No part of this book may be reproduced in any form or by any electronic or mechanical means, including information storage and retrieval systems, without permission in writing from the publisher. If you find facts you know are in error, please drop a note to the author at 936 E. 2nd St., Whitefish, MT 59937.

Library of Congress Catalog Card Number 96-061579

ISBN 0-9645477-8-3
10 9 8 7 6 5 4 3 2 1

Printed in the United States of America
Designed and typeset by Diane Hokans.
Front cover: "Beautiful Skiing Background" photo by Marion Lacy courtesy Mike Muldown. Pictured (left to right) are Ernie Hileman, Jim Caughren, Lloyd Muldown and Tige Roulette ca. 1937. Antique skis courtesy Martha York. Antique ski poles courtesy Mike Muldown. Antique ski and ski pole photography by Thomas Harrop.
Back cover: photo of The Big Mountain © Thomas Harrop, 1996. Big Mountain goat patch courtesy Sandi Unger. Ptarmigan and Ski School patches courtesy Nancy Hayes.

P.O. Box 4763
Whitefish, MT 59937
(800) 893-0963
(406) 862-9678

Herringbone up the mountain circa 1937.

Acknowledgements

I'd like to thank the 140 people who participated in interviews and provided materials for this book. Additionally, I'd like to thank the following people for their extra efforts in making this book a reality:

Anne Shaw Moran

Lyle Rutherford

Mike Muldown

Stella Matt

Phyllis Prentice

Mary Anne Schenck Miles

Mike Catena

Chet Powell

Marguerite Schenck

Mary Tombrink Harris

Jane Seely Solberg

Introduction

Creating this book became an adventure through the memories of three generations of skiers. Although time challenged memories to recount specific dates, names, or exacting details, the skiers reached consensus on one point. Retired railroader Lyle Rutherford once told me, "You meet up with old friends up there skiing on The Big Mountain. It's a different class of people — outdoors people — not sitting-on-a-bar-stool type people. I'm real proud of it." Among the 140 people I interviewed for this anniversary reminiscence, none disagreed with Rutherford. The Big Mountain was and is a meeting place of friends. And if some of those friends are absent from the chutes, schusses and glades, my hope is that they will meet up again, if not on the slopes, perhaps on these pages.

~ *Jean Arthur*

Opposite: Cal Tassinari in the Big Drift area, early 1960s.

1

Hellroaring

 In the depression-poor years of the 1930s, a carload of young Whitefish adventurers pooled their nickels for gasoline. They drove a Model A Ford coupe to the end of a snow-covered trace. Wearing leather boots, wool slacks and hand-knit sweaters, they strapped on handmade wooden skis outfitted with fur-skinned climbers for uphill travel. These skiing pioneers began a winter tradition on what has become Montana's sterling showpiece, The Big Mountain.

From 1933 until the United States requested their presence in the War in 1941, a handful of skiers had the mountains to themselves. They climbed past Whitey's cabin on a road that Whitey Henderson made with the help of a pick ax. Scrappy, energetic and adventurous, these explorers mustered their way up to the burns, glades and bowls of the biggest mountain in the peaks.

Some of the earliest skiers, Ole Dalen and Lloyd "Mully" Muldown, met while exploring the Whitefish Range. "Ole skied with his stepfather on homemade skies using one ski pole held horizontally with both hands," recounts Sugar Dalen, Ole's widow.

Mully brought a pair of maple skis out to the little Montana outpost of Whitefish when he moved from his native Minnesota in 1928.

Opposite: Ole Dalen in powder.
Upper right: Karl Hinderman and Lloyd "Mully" Muldown bring suitcases and packs into the Hell-Roaring cabins.

"I was brought up in a Norwegian community," said Mully in a 1986 interview. "We had little jumps. Many people were making skis out of maple and ash for cross-country and jumping. No downhill, period."

He first skied in Whitefish by hanging onto ropes behind cars—skijoring. He often joined friends for skiing on a hill at Spencer Lake. Then, "Some of us got to venturing up on the mountain in 1933. I met Ole Dalen up there one day. He was coming down when I was going up. We were trying to find ways to go up the mountain and come down — a great adventure. Whitey's Mine (below the big switchback at Eagle's Nest on Big Mountain Road) was as far as you could go in winter. When we first started, there was no way we could drive a car up there. We had to climb a great distance breaking trail the whole way."

To get above tree line took a sweaty four hours or more.

"The greatest experience came in '34 when we did get to the top of the mountain one day," said Mully. "And of course that was a big deal because we had to climb a great distance, breaking trail, just two of us, Ole and I."

Big air for Ole Dalen, circa 1938.

Postcard of the Whitefish Ski Club Cabin

During the summer of 1935, while Adolf Hitler developed the Luftwäffe an ocean away, Whitefish volunteers built the first cabin on the mountain in the headwaters of Hell Roaring Creek. Dalen, Muldown, Dr. George Johnson, Chuck Creon, Lyle Rutherford, Tom Dempsey, Bill and Bob Adams, Tige Roulette, Betty Jennings (Muldown), Helen Collins and others organized the Hell-Roaring Ski Club. Their cabin, built not in the present Village area, but higher, near today's Ranger Run between Chair Three and Chair Two, became their winter bivouac, housing eight people in four bunks, all warmed by a barrel stove.

Hell-Roaring, Whitefish Lake and Big Mountain

When the Hell-Roaring Ski Club formed in 1937, the dozen members had no idea that they would leave an endowment of service, fund raising and fun. The club organized loosely at first, with Mully Muldown as president and Lyle Rutherford as secretary.

Soon Hell-Roaring members sponsored races and social events, raised money for racers, and saw that young racers had the opportunity to travel. In 1945, prior to incorporation of Winter Sports, Inc. (WSI), club members changed the name to Whitefish Lake Ski Club at the urging of townspeople with delicate sensibilities. Says Lyle Rutherford, "Some of the people didn't like the name 'Hell-Roaring' so we changed the name."

The Whitefish Lake Ski Club held box-lunch socials, dances and summer picnics, all the while volunteering on ski races and other events. By 1949, the 100 active skiers and 700 associate members included Olympic skiers Gene Gillis, Rhona (Wurtele) Gillis and Toni Matt, and claimed to be the largest ski club in Montana.

ALPINE CLUB PATCH COURTESY JESSIE HARRING

In 1976, after club interest had faded, the club again changed its name to Big Mountain Ski Club and filed Articles of Incorporation as a domestic nonprofit corporation with the State of Montana. The 250 members raise money at their annual Ski Swap and offer financial support to Flathead Valley Ski Foundation, (the fund-raising arm of the Big Mountain Race Team) Special Olympics, DREAM, the WART bus, and for a college scholarship.

Members since 1970, Don and Jessie Harring still volunteer for club events along with Sally Porcarelli, a member since 1971 and club secretary for 20 years.

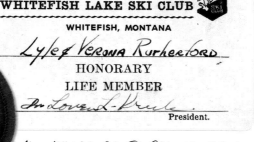

Above: Whitefish Lake Ski Club patch with the skiing devil; Honorary Life Member Lyle Rutherford's Whitefish Lake Ski Club card. Left: Whitefish Lake Ski Club patch for the 1990s

"When we first started, it was alpine and cross country," recalls Porcarelli. "The club put together the Holbrook Picnic Area along Big Mountain Road in the 1970s, cleared it, put in a table and a road all by volunteer hands. It's now maintained by the U.S. Forest Service."

Much of the club's efforts focused on race support, from national events to local Pro-Am City League.

"One night during the Wednesday night league races, we lost the race results," recalls Donna Davis, who grew up skiing The Big Mountain and now gives a little back by volunteering. "Lani Johnson had put the results sheet on the counter in the Bierstube's kitchen, and it slipped down between the wall and the back of the counter."

"We were frantic," says Johnson, remembering asking Stube owner Gary Elliott if they could drill holes in his counter to retrieve the results. "The racers kept asking about the results. We kept telling them, 'Just another minute.'"

"We finally drilled several holes in the back of the cupboard and took two pencil erasers and worked the paper up the wall," says Davis. "Lani got a Frabert for that."

Top right: Whitefish Lake Ski Club patch designed in the 1940s by Gerald Monegan.

Photomontage of Lloyd 'Mully' Muldown circa 1950.

Mully 1906–1993

Early eight-millimeter films show Lloyd Muldown and friends gliding over snow more like ungainly toddlers than smooth athletes. They careened down sheep trails barely staying upright on their seven-foot boards. Technique involved stooping low over the front of skis. Mully, who became known as the "Father of Skiing" on The Big Mountain, first skied as a youngster in Minnesota. When he moved West, he brought skis and a Norseman's appreciation for winter adventure.

"When he got off the train in East Glacier after leaving humid Minnesota and crossing the hot plains, Dad got on the boardwalk, and he said he'd never smelled clean, cool fresh air like that," says Mully's son, Mike. "Right then, he knew he'd never go back."

Enamored with skiing, Mully ventured to Europe in 1936 to watch the Berlin Olympics and to find the latest ski and mountain-climbing equipment, clothing and techniques. His collection of black and white films show the dapper European influence: a spiffy hat the kids called an ear brassiere, fast "dope" (wax) and smooth turns where skiers leaned into a curve known as the Arlberg style. Of course they had climbed up the mountain from East Lakeshore, and so they wore their climbing skins like bandoleers, crisscrossed over their shoulders.

Always the educator, Mully shared his alpine expertise with others. After the war, he coached the high school ski team. In 1972, he retired as Whitefish School Superintendent and joined the Martin Hale Ski School, where he taught until 1989. He served on the board of directors of WSI from 1984 to 1993.

"As a kid, I'd ski with Mully as much as anyone," recalls Ed Gilliland, who later published many photographs of skiers on The Big Mountain. "He always wore his big overcoat. He'd make four or five turns then watch people go by. We'd stop and talk, but he always wanted me to go on ahead. He didn't understand that I was there for the conversation."

Even after Mully no longer trusted his eyes to find trails on The Big Mountain, he continued to ski a mountain that he'd come to know as a friend and where he made friends.

"I remember Mully waiting for bright sunny days because he could see better," says Ridie Armstrong, who ski patrolled in the 1980s and became a professional ski instructor in the 1990s. "He would ski all the main runs. I'd find him part way down Toni Matt Run or on Chair Seven. He skied with his feet and felt the terrain, how it undulated. He would get a sense of where he was on the mountain and let gravity pull him downhill."

Mully spent 80-some years of his life skiing and 44 years teaching, coaching and administrating in Whitefish Schools. Namesakes Lower and Upper Mully's on the mountain and Muldown School showcase the life of a man who exemplified adventure and fortitude and was *rara avis*, one in a million.

Betty Muldown on the top of Hell-Roaring Ski Course in the late 1930s.

That winter the men and women relished the excursion, making their way up Friday evenings and staying through Sunday afternoons.

"In '37, we spent a wonderful winter up there," recalled Lyle Rutherford, a retired conductor for the Great Northern Railway. "There was no work for us downtown, so Ole and I just moved up there and skied on the mountain. We'd cut wood and ski — there was just too much to do to ever get lonely."

Maybe they weren't lonely but by week's end, they were hungry.

"About Friday we hoped somebody would come up with a pack sack of food," says Rutherford. "We ran out of food one Thursday, so Friday we headed to town. When we got to Whitey's, here come a big group heading up. We took the pack sacks off the girls and oh, we had a feast."

Untracked glades kept these vanguards happy. Forest fires of 1910 and 1919 cleared the slopes of brush and trees. Up they'd track, Mully, Rutherford, Dalen and others, above the cabin along the mountain's shoulder.

"It was fabulous skiing because there was no timber," said Rutherford. "We never skied into the hole where the lodges are today because we'd have had to climb out."

According to Mully, local clergy caught wind of men and women slumbering in the same cabin and proclaimed that turpitude would not be tolerated. Other skiers suggested the group needed larger quarters for the burgeoning sport. So during the summer of 1938, Rutherford, Dalen, Chuck Creon, and Tige Roulette built another cabin, this one larger with vertical logs to brace the roof against heavy snow accumulation.

Using horses to snake logs to the building site, the volunteers spent the summer building a clubhouse for a new ski club, Hell-Roaring.

"Hell, I'd never driven a horse before," recalls Tige Rolette. "So I just hooked Old Silver's single tree up with a half-hitch around a log and tried to keep up. The log would skid down steep slopes onto the horse's legs, so most of my job was keeping out of the way."

Otto Ost circa 1938.

What a stinking mess!

"After I graduated from high school in 1941, and after I had obtained gainful employment at a local clothing store, I invested in my first pair of skis — wooden with real metal edges that came in about six-inch sections, each locked into adjacent edge, and held onto the skis' grooved-out edge with myriad tiny screws which, if one were lucky, stayed in place for at least one weekend," said Otto Ost.

During the week, skiers built up new bases on their fancy skis.

"Everybody would be putting on new edges, ironing in layers of pine-tar, and later, scraping off all the old lacquer and building layer after layer of new base. Some of my friends endeared themselves forever in the hearts of their mothers by borrowing her electric iron to properly prepare the base of their skis with the blackish-brown layer of pine tar! What a stinking mess — but it was important that our skis slid properly!"

Marion Lacy

Equipped with a German Linhoff four-by-five and a Kodak Medalist 620, Marion Lacy ventured into the mountains during storms to await the crisp, clear light that would follow a squall. Soft-spoken, tall and lean, the photographer produced thousands of black and white photographs of Northwest Montana.

"I met Marion Lacy in 1946 when I started the *Hungry Horse News*," recalls Mel Ruder. "He saved my bacon more than once. I never had the darkroom technique, so Lacy made my prints through the years. He was an expert photo-finisher, well recognized in the state."

Lacy and his wife Etta held posts as Glacier National Park fire lookouts in the summers. Before The Big Mountain opened in 1947, he often attached climbing skins to skis and scaled the peak to make photographs.

"The first time I skied to the top of the mountain was in 1945 when I was 13 years old," recalls Gary Tallman. "There was someone ahead of us, breaking trail. We caught up to Marion Lacy and his brother. He was on the way to take pictures. Together we hiked the rest of the way to the top. We took off our climbers and skied down. Marion Lacy left his climbers on and hiked down. I couldn't believe that someone would do that."

Skiers Bill Adams, Danny Hinderman, Bill Hunt, unknown skier, and Marion Lacy.

"Fantasy Forest, The Big Mountain Ski Area" postcard circa 1950.

That Lacy seemed a poor skier shouldn't surprise anyone. Loaded with 40 pounds of expensive photographic equipment, Lacy took time to make award-winning photographs of the snowghosts.

"No one had ever seen pictures of the snowghosts," says Tallman. "Of course, Marion Lacy made them well-known."

He broke a leg skiing one year, yet hobbled around the mountains using a sled for his casted leg and still made photographs.

Looking to trim weight from his pack, Lacy meticulously reconstructed a Graflex camera.

"He used an odd-sized film, a 3¼ by 4¼ film," says Ralph Burtsfield, Lacy's protégé who eventually bought Lacy's studio in 1976. "He rebuilt the Graflex for hiking and climbing. He was truely a master cameraman."

Marion Ernest Lacy died in his Arizona home in 1980.

Tenured Skiers

While Mully and Ole Dalen were most certainly the first skiers to the top of The Big Mountain in 1934, two women — Laura Jo Forhan Measure and Marian Callahan — were probably the first Kalispell women to ski The Big Mountain. And Measure's husband, Ambrose, has laid tracks on the mountain for 60 years.

"I skied up there in 1936-37," recalls "Jo" Measure. "Marian and I, and Ambrose Measure joined the Whitefish bunch, Mully, Ole and the whole group. It was quite a climb to get up there, but we tried to go up every weekend as soon as we were through with work."

This photo of Laura Jo Forhan Measure graced the cover of the Great Northern GOAT magazine circa 1937.

After the skiers built the first Hell-Roaring cabin, they often stayed the weekend.

"The girls had the loft," says Jo. "We had to hike up, and by the time we got to the cabin, nobody had energy left for shenanigans, just the energy to fix a hot tea."

She tells of ski clothes, mostly Army-surplus woolies and hand-me-downs. Jo notes that the quality and style of clothes didn't add much warmth to either relationships or to perspiring skiers, "so we didn't spend much time standing around saying cute things and flirting."

Yet theirs was a romance made for the curvaceous and sometimes rocky slopes of the mountains. Together they'd forge through brush and deep snow to reach the Hell-Roaring cabin, Ambrose in the lead.

"I remember going up one night, beating up through the brush because there were no trails yet, and I lagged behind," she says. "Ambrose said, 'You know you must make it all the way because I can't carry you.' And he'd say things like 'I saw a big bear track.' I'd want to turn around, but he wouldn't, so I'd plod along."

Ambrose, who started skiing at Essex in 1932 or '33, remembers his first skis, "a pair of pine Northlands, nine feet long, from the Kalispell Mercantile for nine dollars."

Climbing skins or "climbers," as they were known, were not yet available in Kalispell, so Jo made climbers out of canvas.

"I knit his ski socks and mittens out of real fine yarn too," she adds, laughing. "He said that I knit warts into them because they were not as smooth as store-bought ones."

At the Hell-Roaring Ski Club Cabin in 1936 are Karl Hinderman, Laura Jo Forhan (Measure), Harold "Bud" Dalen, Ambrose Measure.

They married anyway in 1940. The Measures skied together for many years. Following an injury, Jo took up cross-country skiing. Ambrose, whose 89th birthday coincides with The Big Mountain's 50th birthday, is a season-pass holder, skis every wintry Thursday, and in the off-season, hikes in Glacier National Park.

"I have mixed feelings about the development up there," says Ambrose. "When we used to go up, it was isolated and you had the feeling of having things to yourself. You depended upon your own body to get you up the mountain and get down."

The Name Game

As the story goes, The Big Mountain's promoters stumbled upon the name "The Big Mountain" simply because Mully Muldown pointed up to the peak he dearly loved to ski and called it "that big mountain." The name stuck. Other names have not.

In early literature about the Hell-Roaring Ski Club, the club's name is most often hyphenated; however, the local press often ignored the hyphen. Various maps from the U.S. Forest Service to local promotional fliers wrote it as one word: Hellroaring.

Otto Ost recalled that in 1941, when chairlifts were non-existent, he and his friends herring-boned up "Haskill Mountain," their name for The Big Mountain.

Sometimes the innocuous name The Big Mountain, "Where Big is our middle name," as the brochures state, causes confusion and frustration for people marketing the ski area. Some proposed calling it Hellroaring again, while others offered new names. In the mid 1980s, a marketing manager suggested changing the name to "Legendary." The parking lot would become a fenced stockade, he proposed, and the ski patrol would be outfitted in buckskins and coon-skin caps. No legend or official name change followed.

When The Big Mountain prepared for the 1949 National races, few runs had official names.

"The National Championship slalom will be set on 'Mully's Mile,' over a course of approximately 2,600 feet with a vertical drop of about 900 feet," reads the race program. Mully's Mile was renamed Main Slope in the 1950s, and Ed's Run in later years. The 1949 downhill course from the top of The Big Mountain was named Langley's Run after National Ski Association President Roger Langley. Some of the run is still called Langley's.

For a time, a spot near the top of the old T-bar was called Muldown's Mound. Trail names that have gone the way of beartrap bindings and 25-cent beer include Satan's Descent, Canonan Schuss, Dipsy Doodle, Tipsy Doodle, Suicide Trail, Heinke's Hassle, School Run and Hartson's Highway.

A 1960 edition of the WHITEFISH PILOT tells of the renaming of a beginner run: "By popular demand, the name of the beginner slope has been changed from the former Dope Slope. Now it's Hope Slope. Do you feel better?"

Originally the chairlifts were numbered Chair One, Two, Three, etc., but in the early 1980s, the lifts were renamed. Chair One became Going-to-the-Sun then the Quad Glacier Chaser; Chair Two became Hellroaring; Chair Three, Tenderfoot; Chair Four, Great Northern; Chair Five, Glacier View; Chair Six, Village Lift; and Chair Seven, North Slope. The names stuck, at least on official trail maps.

Not on the official maps but certainly popular powder shots include Slingshot, Mary's Apron, Movieland, Chicken Ridge, The Tubes and Lone Pine. Favorite intermediate areas Hogan's and Hogan's East are named for Steve Hogan who died in 1979 on the mountain after a day of powder skiing. On Hogan's final run he fell into a tree well and suffocated.

Snowghost early 1940s.

The Broken Ski Tree

"We called that trail 'Nose Dive,'" recalls Frank Gregg, who skied the mountain during the Hell-Roaring days. "That was just after the road was built in 1940 or '41. We skied straight down, jumping the road several times on the route to town."

Such was the turn on Nose Dive, a real cranky sort of crick in the trail where more skiers plowed snow with their noses than nosed past the compressed bend.

"My first and second pairs of skis lost mates there on Nose Dive," he says. Those days, wooden skis were 'haute couture' yet wilted as easy as a snowflake in August.

"We nailed 'em to the Ski Tree, an old pine. I heard the skis still hang there today, somewhere below the Village area near the private land. Used to be lots of busted skis nailed to trees."

Finished by fall, the new hut was a mountain Taj Mahal fitted with luxuries like outdoor plumbing, a wood cook stove and two lofts.

"The gals had bunks on this side," Chuck Creon waves his hand, "and the guys on the other side. The extra guys slept on the porch. We'd move the ladder once the guys were in bunks so as nobody could do any sneakin' around. In the morning, we'd climb up to top of mountain and ski down. In the afternoon, we'd crank up the old rope tow. We used to go up east of the cabins, back up hill and ski up there."

Creon and others had hauled a tow rope mechanism up the mountain on horseback that summer of '38 for the Hell-Roaring Ski Club members, many of whom, like Creon, worked for the Great Northern Railway. The year prior, the U.S. Forest Service issued the club a Special-Use Permit for their mechanized activities.

"We had two or three Model T Ford wheels strapped on trees up there," says Creon. "We run the rope down those, had an A-frame down there with a wheel in it. The rope went around the wheel and up to the power unit up above. Fred Hotel built the thing. Had an old car with an engine my dad had.

Above: Joseph Franklin Kincaid snowshoed with a representative from Montana Power Company to the top of Big Mountain before 1947.

Left: Ole Dalen, pioneer of skiing in Whitefish. He does a "gelandesprung," or land jump.

10 HELLROARING *Fifty Years on The Big Mountain*

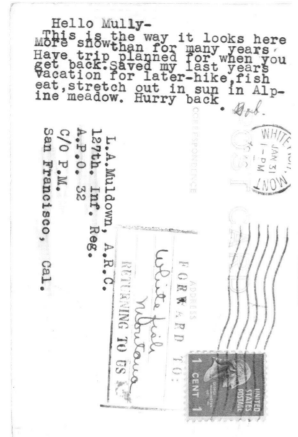

Wartime postcard to Lloyd Muldown from his brother-in-law Bub Jennings.

"We took that and a transmission and an old Dodge frame. The transmission was behind that. A guy had a Willy's Knight car front end and mounted it on a frame. Fred took parts and welded spider gears together and with a regular rear end of a car, the wheels turned."

After weekend frolics, they skied their eight-foot hickories down to town on Sunday evenings.

"The climax of our weekend was to ski down the trail," says Rutherford. "Even after the road went in in 1939, we'd jump the road and ski down Whitey's trail. Ol' Whitey was as sociable as a spotted pup. He had a lime mine back in the hills, and he sold lime to various people. We used his trail — that's where the power line goes up now."

When the United States entered World War II, the intrepid skiers found themselves far from the idyllic mountains of Whitefish. Ole Dalen, Karl Hinderman and Otto Ost joined the famed Tenth Mountain Division, the mountain troops who patrolled the Italian Alps on skis. While the war effort jump-started the economy, for the better part of a decade, the Hell-Roaring Ski Club cabins sat empty.

2
Winter Sports Incorporates

Opposite: Lloyd Muldown, Ed Schenck and Prince, the dog, looking at The Big Mountain with Russell Street, April, 1947.

"The morning after I got to town, a committee decked out in coonskin caps and snowshoes took me up to inspect the skiing country, firsthand," recounted Schenck. "They were as eager to please as rental agents in a ghost town."

Upper right: The Big Mountain embroidered patch from the 1970s.

The dust from World War II had barely settled when the Whitefish Chamber of Commerce began courting winter tourism. The Great Northern Railway surveyors scouted for the perfect ski hill to rival Sun Valley, the prima donna of Averell Harriman's Union Pacific Railroad.

In March 1946, "ski experts" traveled to Whitefish on behalf of the Great Northern Railway. Al Lindley, Earling Strom and others explored potential ski terrain, but it wasn't until Mully took them into Glacier National Park and Heaven's Peak that they found their Grail. Lindley, a member of the 1932 Olympic Team, knew that a ski area in the Northern Rockies could be profitable, so he went to Washington D.C. soliciting the Department of the Interior for permission to build a ski area at Heaven's Peak inside Glacier National Park. Permission was denied.

Heartbroken to hear that their Hell-Roaring haven was "God-forsaken bush country," as Earling Strom described Whitefish's mountain to Muldown, promoters looked elsewhere for support.

Thus it was with great enthusiasm that the Chamber of Commerce embraced Ed Schenck and George Prentice in early 1947. The Great Falls pair had searched the West for an ideal location to begin a ski area.

"George and Ed had been looking around in the Sierras, around Lake Tahoe way back then," recalls Phyllis Prentice, George's wife.

"But the land was terribly expensive."

Having worked for Constam T-bar lifts as salesmen, they knew what to look for. And what they'd found in Whitefish — an enthusiastic community with railway transportation — could lead to success.

After their visit to the mountain, the February 4, 1947 edition of the *Whitefish Pilot* reported: "Hell-Roaring Ski Course Has Championship Possibilities. Whitefish has a chance of becoming a second 'Sun Valley.' After an inspection of Hell Roaring Ski Course on Hell Roaring Mountain, C.E. Schenck, committee chairman of the National Ski Association and the Rocky Mountain Ski Association, adjudged the course as having the finest possibilities for the many departments of the sport, of any course in the Northwest area."

Prentice and Schenck began with $20,000 of their own investment, a beat-up Jeep and a wealth of inspiration. They convinced the Chamber to raise another $40,000, and on March 31, 1947, they formed Winter Sports, Inc. (WSI). Some $70,000 worth of stock went on sale at $100 to $200 a share.

Under the Board of Directors of Schenck, Prentice, Brad Seely and Bill Cripe, The Big Mountain Ski Resort was born. Yet 1947 proved to be a wet, muddy experience. Prentice cut trees and mowed brush for the Ski Lodge, using a D-7 Cat to tackle tamaracks.

"It didn't stop raining until it started snowing," George Prentice later told his grandson, Noah Closson.

The Ski Lodge, built by Schenck and Prentice with help from Chuck Creon, George Savage, Joe Ward and others, formed the basis for today's Village area.

"Ed had Joe Ward and me gather all the rocks for the fireplace from all over the

Above: Original Ski Lodge in construction 1947. The Main Slope and T-bar in back. ABELL PHOTO *Top right: Ed Schenck plowing the road to the Lodge in 1947. Bottom right: Building the T-bar in 1947. George Savage is in the foreground.*

mountain by hand," recalls Savage, who says it took a couple weeks to drag sleds full of rocks to the building site.

For Schenck, Prentice and their crew, spring, summer and fall became a scramble of construction, maintenance and promotion. The first employees — Bob Adams, Gub Akey, Pete Ducy, Bill Hunt and Reg MacDonald — dug out the path for the T-bar.

"We started clearing brush for the slope where Chair Two is now," says Reg MacDonald. "Ed paid us $1.25 an hour, really pretty good at the time." Kids like Gary Tallman cleared the slopes of brush.

"The first T-bar was all hand-dug by local kids hired by Ed Schenck," says Tallman.

Raising Interest

The WHITEFISH PILOT reported on February 7, 1947, that two Great Falls men gave the Whitefish Lions Club a verbal resumé of the "advantages of all-around skiing in this section, and Hell Roaring Mountain in particular, over nearly every other location in the western part of the United States."

When Ed Schenck and George Prentice arrived in Whitefish that winter, together they had $20,000. Through efforts of Brad Seely, president of the Chamber of Commerce, few businessmen escaped without buying stock in WSI. As Ed Schenck told Edmund Christopherson of the SATURDAY EVENING POST, after eight months of "hard labor... the project was dead broke. Everyone in Whitefish, from our creditors to our stockholders, was fed up with the whole affair. It was a community enterprise, and for nearly a year they'd stayed up nights figuring out how to get a ski development under way, selling stock to meet payrolls and even donating their labor to keep things rolling up on the hill."

Seely called a meeting.

"'Anyhow, this is a good place for it to die,' George [Prentice] said in his quiet way, as we slowly climbed the steps to the meeting place over Catron's Funeral Home," continued Schenck.

"There must have been nearly 100 townsfolk sitting around the outside of the hall, and they were the quietest, longest-faced chamber-of-commerce crowd I've ever seen. When it looked as if everyone was there, I noticed that Shirley Lincoln not only closed the doors, he locked them too," continued Schenck.

To Schenck's surprise, Seely positively supported the venture and asked the town to invest more.

"'Do I hear a thousand?' [demanded Seely.] 'Five hundred? Three hundred?' Never in my life had I heard such silence," said Schenck. "For two minutes — it seemed like at least two hours — no one spoke. If Brad had planted any bidders in the crowd to start the ball rolling, they were forgetting their lines. Finally Joe Monegan broke the silence with 'You can put me down for another three hundred.' ...By the time the doors were unlocked more than $6,000 had been subscribed."

Such believers in the future of a ski area were Shirley Lincoln of Lincoln's Cleaners, and Rusty Abell, founder of the Whitefish Credit Union, that they not only knocked on doors to sell stock, but they did it repeatedly when the mountain couldn't make payroll. And when young businessmen couldn't afford to buy stock, Abell loaned them money.

"My business, the Whitefish Taxi Company, was just getting started and I didn't have money to invest," recalls Roy Duff. "So Rusty loaned me the money to buy five shares of stock, at no interest. Five-hundred dollars was a lot of money in 1947."

Financial troubles didn't fade for The Big Mountain. Often Tuesday's payroll was met that day through the efforts of Abell and Lincoln.

"Shirley spent a lot of time on the street selling stock," recalls Lincoln's brother-in-law, Lee Brockel. "He wasn't an active skier. He just liked to get involved and saw it a worthwhile thing to promote doing business in Whitefish."

Not without a bit of humor in the back of his mind did Ed Schenck send Norm Kurtz to town one day with a grocery list.

"I got kicked out of every store in town except Street's and Knott Mercantile," laughs Kurtz, who received his first shares of stock when the mountain couldn't make payroll. "I used to talk to Bernie Hartman at Skyline Dairy: 'Geez, Bernie, just keep us going a few more weeks,' I'd say. He said, 'As long as you tell me what your problem is [in paying the milk bill] and how you're going to fix it, I'll never cut you off.' There were others who helped us survive on credit. For years."

A toast to good skiing! Gladys Creon, George and Phyllis Prentice and Chuck Creon.

"I was younger at the time and ended up doing a lot of brush clearing. We got paid, but years later, everything we did was traded for skiing. We volunteered and just did it."

"The Big Mountain became one of the few ski areas in the country whose genesis was initiated and completed by locals," says Mike Muldown, Mully's son.

Unnamed runs decorated the mountain's face. On December 14, 1947, The Big Mountain opened, but not before some anxious moments. The T-bar, it seemed, had taken on a mind of its own. Skiers became bronc riders.

"The night before the mountain opened, we were up there playing," recalls Lyle Rutherford. He went to ride the T-bar and instead of his skis gliding up the track, suddenly "I was swinging up there like an ape. The darn cable wouldn't let you down. It picked you right up until you were sitting on it like a chicken on a roof with skis dangling below."

Chuck Creon was their best mechanic. He and Schenck went to work and "took a lot of the bugs out of that thing," according to Rutherford. "Opening day, everybody was pretty excited about it. Ride up, ski down, and do it all over again."

Lift tickets that season sold for two dollars. A burger in the Lodge cost twenty-five cents, and a beer was a few nickels. A total of 6,900 skiers enjoyed The Big Mountain that first year, netting the fledgling WSI corporation a loss of $3,600.

By the fall of 1948, Austrian Toni Matt was in Whitefish to design the downhill course for the National Championship races. Having won every national ski race title worth winning, Matt brought the Arlberg style of skiing and his own brand of good humor to The Big Mountain. The little ski area's kismet seemed favorable.

With few ski runs and even fewer lodging opportunities, the bold Winter Sports, Inc. bid to host the

At the snack bar.

1949 National Downhill, Slalom and Combined Championship Ski Races. And won! The successful event focused the national ski fervor on The Big Mountain. WSI investors realized that The Big Mountain would need more financing before they'd see any profit. Shirley Lincoln, of Lincoln's Cleaners, and Rusty Abell, president of the Whitefish Credit Union, convinced skiers and non-skiers alike to purchase stock although naysayers often remarked that the stock would be worthless and campaigned against the mountain.

Riding the T-bar circa 1952.

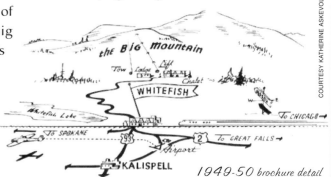

1949-50 brochure detail

"Once a couple of disgruntled stockholders started a movement to have us run out of town," Schenck once said. "Since our project on the hill was largely built with the townsfolk's money, we're watched as closely as…a new schoolteacher."

Ebb Schuehle built the Rocky Mountain Chalet in the summer of 1949, and by the winter of 1951-52, advertised "six days and nights of good skiing and skiing fun for $62."

It was that "skiing fun" that became the signature of The Big Mountain. Mary Anne Schenck Miles, Schenck's eldest daughter, remembers the "skiing fun" as the Bongo Board in front of the Chalet's fireplace where guests, employees and kids tried standing on a board with a roller underneath, rocking like a seesaw. Dave Reitan, who came to teach skiing in 1956, remembers the fun as Fall-Line Hour and skits.

And Gary Tallman sums it up with the pranks by the ski patrol and the ski school.

"I was in the ski school, taught for Toni Matt," recalls Tallman. "We always had a friendly rivalry with the ski patrol. They were a bunch of characters, always playing jokes on each other. Patrol had a big stuffed toy monkey they called Frabert. The ski school members — Dave Reitan, Martin Hale, Jim Black, Bob Nicholas and I — decided to steal Frabert."

Not Alone

Since the mid 1930s, ski areas cropped up across the nation. In cooperation with the U.S. Forest Service, Sun Valley became the first winter sport area on national forest land in 1936, leading the way for hundreds of ski clubs like Hell-Roaring to open slopes to the public.

Hell-Roaring Ski Club was not alone in the Flathead Valley. By 1941, a small ski hill with a rope tow operated on national forest land outside Belton (West Glacier).

Termaat's Ski Area envelope advertising their two-rope tow hill outside Kalispell near Lake Blaine. "Basically we were farmer-ranchers, and had tractors, so we used the two rubber tired ones to power the tows," said Harold Termaat. "The ticket was 50 cents for the one or a dollar for the other tow — you could ski on either tow for the dollar. We rented the outfit, skis, poles and boots for $1.75."

Kalispell's Silver Buckle Ski course operated in 1959 by Ed Nordtome had a small ski tow about three miles south of town. Frenchy's "Little Mountain" operated in the 1960s through the early '70s, across U.S. 93 from the Par 3 on 93 golf course in Whitefish. And a Creston family operated a commercial ski slope with a rope tow during the 1950s.

"I had two tows and two John Deeres going at the same time," says Harold Termaat of his farm-side slopes near Lake Blaine. "We got 50 cents for the small hill and a dollar for the big hill. Parents said it was the cheapest baby sitting they could find."

He ran his rope tows from the late '50s through '68, then sold his rope "to a guy who wanted to start a new ski hill somewhere."

All but The Big Mountain have closed.

All Day for $1.25. Riding the rope tow 1950.

After retiring from the railroad, Frank "Grandpa Mac" MacDonald ran the rope tow and used to say, "I wiped 10,000 noses, put on 20,000 mittens and tucked 1,000 pigtails."

Left: The new Tucker Snocat purchased in 1956 for $8,000. Photo includes Pacific Power & Light official, Norm Kurtz, Lyman Oliver, Ed Schenck in driver's seat, a representative from Pacific Power & Light, Karl Hinderman and Red Harding.

"We could pull ten people behind the Tucker on ropes, and four or five inside for a ride to the top of the mountain," recalls Kurtz.

Above: Tucker Sno-Cat and Trailer. Ed Schenck in Cat.
Lower left and insert: On the ski school bus.
Below: University of Montana skiers on the balcony of the Ski Lodge during the college club's ski weekend.

On one of the balconys of the Ski Lodge University of Montana skiers take time off for coffee.

Downtown Whitefish as shown in a 1949-50 Big Mountain brochure.

George Prentice 1909 — 1993

"The fellas didn't have much time to even spend time with their families in those first years of The Big Mountain," recalls Phyllis Prentice.

"I'd take our daughter, Jan, up to the mountain and visit. Jan was walking around and any tall skiing blonde fellow she'd see, she'd run up and throw her arms around him, and call him 'Daddy,' much to the embarrassment of several young men."

George Prentice was born in Great Falls and grew up skiing King's Hill. After World War II, he and Ed Schenck teamed resources and enthusiasm to open a new ski hill.

After six years on the mountain and summers working on the Hungry Horse Dam project, Prentice accepted a position with an engineering firm.

"The mountain couldn't support Ed and his family in any fashion in those days," recalls Phyllis. "Ed had married a local girl, and her family was already here. George was offered another job, so when we had the opportunity to leave, we did."

He spent the next 23 years estimating engineering projects for a New York company before retiring and returning to The Big Mountain.

"I retired from teaching school, and we moved back to Whitefish," says Phyllis. "Ed asked George to take over ticket checking, and soon he took over ticket sales. I worked as cashier and hostess at the Ptarmigan Room for five years before I went to work for Martin and Greta Hale in the ski shop."

Whitefish resident Diana McKeen Arnot skiing in 1951.

George Prentice stringing communications line for a race.

"George would tell us stories about ski packing the slopes in those early years," says Elaine White who worked for George in the ticket office. "Those were his glory years. His eyes would light up when he'd talk about the early days on the mountain. He took a great amount of pride in establishing the mountain."

Since Prentice enjoyed the snow on the mountain's North Slope during the last few years he skied, The Big Mountain honored his service to the skiers of Montana by dedicating George's Gorge on the North Slope to George Prentice.

Ed Schenck 1914 — 1982

Ed Schenck, a mountain of a man, spent 18-hour days creating The Big Mountain. A hard working, intelligent and gentle man, he was known as a frugal employer. He also had the respect of his employees.

"We used to work hard for Ed," recalls George Savage, who helped build the Lodge in 1947. "But it was a funny thing. We'd get him telling war stories and sit around all afternoon, and I'd never move a hand."

Phyllis Prentice, wife of Schenck's partner, agrees.

"A real raconteur," says Phyllis Prentice, who recalls her first meeting with Schenck. "He came to our house for dinner, and we stayed up all night listening to his wonderful stories."

The Great Falls native foresaw a future in skiing as both a business and a family recreation. After searching the West for just the right mountain to create a ski area, he found in Whitefish the magic combination of mountains, rails, and boosters. His impressions of the mountain were recounted in a 1987 article in *Montana Magazine*.

"'When we finally struggled to the top, we found breathtaking, vast open snowfields where you could ski in any direction, southern slopes, seven-foot-deep snow topped by soft powder, and sunshine — all the things a skier dreams about,' said Schenck. 'Beautiful snow-laden evergreens loomed against the rock-topped blue ranges of Glacier National Park, twenty miles to the east.'"

If he'd worn a name tag, it would have read "General Manager." His duties, however, were

Opposite: Ed Schenck skiing, winter of '47-48.

Ed and Marguerite Schenck clowning around, 1957. "It was just before Christmas," recalls Marguerite. "We'd stored the kids' gifts at a friend's and when we went to pick them up, Ed and I rode the kiddie car across the front porch."

much less glamorous: ditch-digger, brush-cutter, tractor driver, carpenter and road builder.

Schenck found himself so busy that he had little time to enjoy the skiing although all five of his children skied. Instead, says his widow Marguerite, he found satisfaction in his job which he always said was his hobby.

"In the course of one day, Ed loaded the lift, tended bar, cooked burgers, patrolled the slopes and plowed the road," says Schenck's grandson, Jeremy Miles. "For many years, he was the only true full-time employee on The Big Mountain. This left him with little time to spend with his family and friends, and it seemed he and his family were always in debt. He didn't have the simple pleasures that others enjoy. He was on the verge of failure for many years, but not once did he ever capitulate. Although it was probably 30 years before he began making any profit, he never gave up his dream even when others doubted the possibility of his success. The mountain can truly attribute most of its early success to Ed Schenck's determination."

From a few scratched runs into a mountain's hardy side to a half-dozen lifts, chalets, restaurants and shops, Schenck's vision propelled Whitefish into an elite club of nationally renowned resorts, rated in the Top Ten by many national ski publications.

Unfortunately Schenck died before realizing his dream of a Summit House at 7,000 feet. Yet as his Big Mountain passes its gold anniversary, Schenck is remembered for his flair of a statesman and his spirit of adventure.

A Stay at the Chalet

"They'd wake you up in the morning by playing chimes while walking down the hallway announcing breakfast," recalls Kitty Jones, whose family flew from Billings in 1962 for a week's vacation after her father Bruce Anderson read an article about The Big Mountain in the *Saturday Evening Post*.

"My parents loved The Big Mountain and the Chalet because we kids could come and go as we pleased, and because the Chalet had the American Plan in the restaurant. They just laid out the food, and we could pick out whatever we wanted."

The dining was elegant, the lodging romantic, and the skiing challenging. A Chalet room for four people went for ten dollars a night, or the American Plan Package including room, all meals, lifts and twelve ski school lessons in one week for $78.00 per person.

Jones and her ten-year-old twin brother, David Anderson, roamed the slopes like a pair of ponies cut loose.

"My brother had a great imagination," says Jones. "One day there was a lot of fog in Ptarmigan Bowl. He got the great idea of tying us together with a rope. One of us skied down until the rope was tight, then waited until the other skied down. That's how we got down through the fog."

Above: 1949-50 brochure.

Left: front and back of postcard dated March 13, 1950 to friends in Seattle reads:

"Hi! What do you think of the new Chalet. Gee – I wish you could be here on a Sunday – you wouldn't know the place. Mobs of people and worse now since the article in the [Saturday Evening] Post. When are you coming. Rocky"

From Ski Bum to President and General Manager: Norm Kurtz

He claims to have the strongest armpits in the West.

"It's from riding rope tows all those years," says Norm Kurtz, a Washington native who discovered The Big Mountain in 1951 during a break from college. "I never had any money for ski passes, so to get a pass, I started hauling gas in a Jeep can in a backpack up the rope tows [which were powered by gasoline engines] at Snoqualmie Pass, [Washington]."

When college break came around, Kurtz and a friend headed for powder skiing in Wyoming, but by the time they got into Spokane, a major winter storm threatened to shut down U.S. Highway 10.

"This is in the days of Warren Miller," says Kurtz. "We had a baby-bottle warmer plugged into the cigarette lighter and hooked it to the steering wheel. That's how we warmed our butterhorns. Oh, we were ski bumming!"

Listening to their portable radio, they heard talk of road closure from the storm.

"We turned at Missoula and went up to this Whitefish place. We pulled into the Palm Bar. This guy says, 'You skiers?' We say, 'Yup.' We never bought a drink that night."

They slept in their car then skied powder the next day.

"That night we were getting ready to sleep in the car again when Dot Overmeyer, the Lodge manager, knocked on our window, told us that we didn't know nothin' about a winter storm until we froze in a Montana storm. So we slept on the floor in the old Lodge. What we didn't know was that there were thirteen girls from Concordia College who had just arrived. From that time forward, we thought we'd died and gone to heaven."

Kurtz finished college then began working for Ed Schenck in 1955. He became General Manager in the late '70s, and worked for the mountain in various capacities until 1991.

"Carolee was the Ski Lodge manager, and I was the mountain assistant manager," recalls Kurtz. "There was no insulation in the Chalet and after a storm I'd actually go up into rooms Six and Seven to shovel out snow that blew in through the seams! I'd keep piling electric heaters up until the fuses would blow, just to make the place habitable."

Norm and Carolee Kurtz managed the Chalet in 1955.

Relaxing around the fire place in the Chalet.

Maiden in the Cold

It was 1958, and two high school boys skied The Big Mountain. Snow hurled itself upon them in clumps like white socks thrown down by some childish giant during a temper tantrum. Gil Harrison and Tom Deatherage met the white cotton with their thighs and chests, their bodies undulating over the ungroomed bumps and snow-covered logs.

Near the bottom they paused, as always, to allow each other room for the traverse, a schussed tuck along a narrow ski track back to the lift. Without momentum, schuss became slog. If a skier steered out of the track, the knee-deep snow worked like a brake slowing the joy out of the ride.

Deatherage jumped into an aerodynamic tuck first. Down the last steep he dove, across the compression and along the flat track, around the bend and home. At least that was the plan. Instead of a clean route, the corner met him with an embrace. There, crouched in the track under the thrown cotton, squatted a woman's bare backside, coloring the snow.

With the swift reaction of growing moss, Deatherage maintained his schuss. He scooped up the body, yellow paint and all, and journeyed down the trail until his unruly lap rider forced an unscheduled stop.

Snow piled upon the tangled skiers.

She, feeling the exact freezing point to the core of her soul on one end and flushing a roasted rouge on the other end, found a melting point all over his black stretch pants.

He, feeling her warmth, dispensed with common courtesy, forgot to introduce himself, and did not help her up.

Harrison, on the other hand, now enjoying the full velocity of the track, schussed past and asked, "What are you doing?"

Deatherage untangled boots and poles and skis. Without a word he skated off leaving the maiden in the cold.

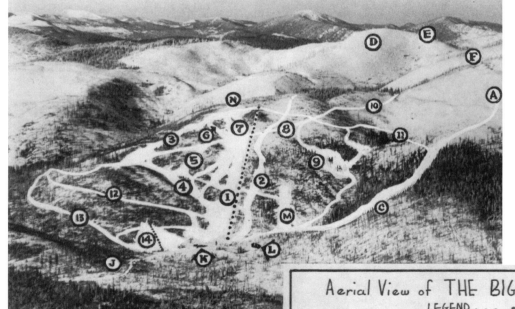

The Big Mountain map circa 1955.

Kalispell Ski Club

In 1957, a handful of Kalispell skiers including Bob Fehlberg, Jim Stephens, and Gail and Oystein Boveng formed the Kalispell Ski Club. What began with a few dozen skiers has grown to 320 family memberships. Kalispell hosts its own Ski Swap and a Saturday Learn-to-Ski program started by Norwegian ski jumper Thor Hauge. Annually 300 kids take club lessons.

"Part of what ski clubs were about was promoting skiing to get local people interested in skiing," says Oystein Boveng, who learned to ski and ski jump in Norway. "We offered free lessons to kids for years."

Pat Gyrion, Kalispell Ski Club's Learn-To-Ski director for 15 years, says that teaching kids to ski brought satisfaction to more than just the kids.

"The club members wanted me to help teach the kids and I told them 'Man, I can barely ski myself.' I was on old Army skis. I paid 20 dollars for them with Cubco bindings, double lace-up boots, and my feet froze in them, and then were immobile for five hours after skiing. You could sharpen those skis and shave with them. I'd cross the slope, stop, do a kick turn, and cross the slope again. But I learned more through the clinics taught by Martin Hale and the ski school and by teaching than by anything else."

"In those days, skiers raced four-way," recalls Jim Stephens, the Kalispell Ski Club's first president and now a lifetime member. "Originally 25 or 30 people organized to be a social club. Then we got into racing and junior programs.

"Thor started the junior racing program. He thought that if we gave them a bit of help with racing, the program would build. Same year that Thor Hauge started, I took the younger bunch. Eventually it became the Junior Ski Program. We wanted to get new skiers involved. Of course if you get kids involved, you get the parents.

"There used to be the Silver Buckle Ranch ski area south of town with Bob Nordtome the owner. Just a rope tow there. A guy named Tap Tapley started a Ladies' Day on Thursdays at Silver Buckle. The gals then got their husbands involved in skiing. It was a good place to learn. Once they got going good they'd go up to Big Mountain. The mountain liked that."

Thor Hauge, Norwegian exchange student and well-known jumper, shown mid-air off The Big Mountain's Class B Jump.

Skiing family, 1958 with John Harrison, Ann Schwartz, Gil Harrison, Jane Schwartz Kohler and Peri Schwartz Shea.

Front and back of 1958 postcard of the Lodge.

Building Chair One

In the spring of 1960, after record snows, the lift line for the new 6,800-foot double chairlift to the top of The Big Mountain had to be plowed out with a D8 cat, a feat, says Norm Kurtz "paled only by the clearing of Logan Pass each spring.

"Came the time to string the inch-and-a-quarter steel cable, we had a hard-working, loyal ex-marine named J.D. Pike, as one of the lead men in the cable pull," says Kurtz. "About the time we had the cable on one of the upper support towers just below the Big Drift, the big wire rope caught on a fallen snag. Pike went to get it loose, and about the time he pulled it away from the snag, the cat pulled on the cable, and up went Pike with the cable, more than 120 feet in the air."

Kurtz says that what Pike retorted as he went up is not printable. "That's why we called it 'B.S. Gulch.' He held on for about five minutes. We lowered him to within 20 feet of the ground before he dropped off, and all he got was a tear in his pants. Toughest guy I ever met."

Building Chair One's Top Terminal. Whitefish Block Company pours the ready mix at footings for top terminal.

After the chairlift towers were in place, they were rigged with sheaves, along which the cable passes. Working here are Bob LeSage, supervising engineer from Heron Engineering Co. Denver, Colorado., designer of the lift, and The Big Mountain's George Murphy.

Aerial view of base area with lift line circling Chair One.

Loading at midway station on old Chair One.

They left a ransom note reading, "If you ever want to see your monkey alive, leave a case of beer at the top of the Poma."

"So the next thing we know," says Tallman, "the patrol stole our ski school bell, tarred and feathered it and rolled it down the bank!" Ransom had not been paid, so the instructors took drastic measures.

"We got hold of a local doctor and had him put Frabert's leg in a big cast," says Tallman. "No case of beer yet, so we put him in a sling with another ransom note saying we were serious. I don't think we ever resolved the ransom, but we returned the monkey."

The Big Mountain became known as a place where guests and guides, friends and Fraberts, had a rocking good time.

"We really tried to entertain the guests, not just ski with them," says Reitan.

Most guests arrived via the Great Northern Railway and stayed for a week. Skiers came in large groups from Minneapolis, Portland, and Seattle, and by the mid '60s, at the height of the ski rails, hundreds of skiers spilled off The Big Mountain and into Whitefish hotels.

"The mountain really 'made it' in 1962, after building the chairlift to the top in 1960," says Norm Kurtz, General Manager in the late 1970s. "By 1959, it had pretty well been figured out that one T-bar, one Poma and one rope tow were just not going to hack it if The Big Mountain was ever going to become a real destination ski resort."

According to Kurtz, two stockholders,

Chair One dedication for 1960-61 ski season. Seated on chair is the Winter Carnival Queen Susan Monroe.

Clarence Knutson and Whit Smith, stepped up to offer cash to build a lift to the top.

"It was relatively big news in the burgeoning ski industry for a little place like Whitefish, Montana, to be building a lift on what they called 'The Big Mountain,' especially since the lift was to be one of the biggest in the U.S.," says Kurtz.

Schenck and the board chose the 6,800-foot-long Heron lift, planted 31 lift towers over a 2,000-foot vertical rise and in December 1960 opened Chair One, one of the longest lifts in the United States at that time.

"The machine worked hard for 28 years [before installation of a high-speed quad]. The first year of Chair One operation, our business went up 141 percent," recalls Kurtz. "We were on our way. That was big time in 1960."

WSI Board of Directors and staff circa 1958 includes Frank Haswell, Ed Schenck, Russell Street, Bob Sullivan, Bill Martin, Norm Kurtz and Jake Heckathorn.

3

Racing: "We're Not Fair-Weather Skiers"

Opposite: 1952 Montana State Champion Girls' Ski Team with coach Mully Muldown, Jane Seely Solberg, Sheila Lacy Morrison, Kaye Simons, Faye McKenzie, and Sharon Hileman.

"One of the team trophies is from Rossland, B.C.," says Solberg, who recalls that 1952 was the first year that the girls' team traveled to Canada. "At that race, Martin Hale didn't enter the jumping competition. Martin hated to jump so I took his place! The announcer said, 'The man jumping number 16 is J. Seely.' Well, I didn't have jumping skis and I fell on the landing. A guy came over and asked if I was okay. He looks at me and yells, 'Hey, it's a she!' The girls' team did better than the boys'."

Upper right: The first ski meet on Hell-Roaring ski slope drew 88 high school racers from around the state in 1939.

Barely had a slope been cleared when Whitefish High School held its first ski tournament in 1939. Betty Muldown recalls that ten schools, 88 kids and 400 spectators hiked to the snowy reaches seven miles from town. The 35 members in the Hell-Roaring Ski Club prepared the course, volunteered for ski patrol and cooked hot lunches for all.

"In 1939 we held the high school state alpine interscholastic meet," recalled Mully Muldown, by then a science teacher and ski coach at the high school. "Everybody had to walk all the way up, all the contestants, the officials, the spectators, *everybody* walked from East Lakeshore. We backpacked all the food. It was crowded."

"Lyle Rutherford was the cook," says Betty Muldown. "I remember he made oatmeal in a wash tub!"

Fifty-three racers and officials crammed into the Hell-Roaring Ski Club cabins. They arduously backpacked belongings some two miles up to Hell-Roaring for the stay. Everyone else stayed in town. Betty Muldown remembered how families housed participants.

Local boys Doug Smith and Duane "Pine Tar" Einan took the trophies in the downhill and slalom, respectively. High schools across the state developed race teams.

"I first raced on the Hell-Roaring ski slope in 1939 on the Neihart Team," says George Savage, who now owns a ski shop in Washington. "In 1941, the state high school championship events were there too. I won

Doug Smith, George Savage and Dan Thorsen in 1941.

Right: John Turmell, Tom Word, and Derrill Smith competed in the Doug Smith Races circa 1955.

Doug Smith 1922–1944

the combined, and Doug Smith was second with Dan Thorson third. Since we ran the course from the top of the mountain, we had to climb up the course then finish down below the old ski club cabins."

On his Northland Ridgetop hickory skis, "really hot stuff – I finally got metal edges in '41," he adds, Savage flew over rough, boot-packed snow. "Mostly, there were very few control gates. We got going pretty fast, 60 or 65 miles per hour."

The second World War idled racing but by 1948, Olympic fever swept the country like an avalanche. The winter Olympics in St. Moritz bestowed upon the world skiing's best athletes. Skiers like Americans Dick Durrance and Gretchen Fraser, and the invincible Toni Matt, the Austrian powerhouse, popularized skiing's chic side.

In 1948, The Big Mountain dedicated the first Doug Smith races as a memorial to the Whitefish racer who had been killed during the war.

"Smith was a real quiet guy," recalls Savage, who went on to win the first two Doug Smith Memorial Races. "Doug and I were on the '41 Montana State Team to Sun Valley to the Jeffers Cup. He had a low ego, not like the athletes of today."

Racing brought skiers, and skiers brought money and national attention. With that in mind, Prentice and Schenck bid to host the 1949 National Ski Association Senior Championships. To many a surprised ski corporation, The Big Mountain won out. That The Big Mountain found itself hosting the championships was another coup for Whitefish promoters.

Course preparation for the downhill began the summer of 1948. Volunteers like Reg MacDonald logged trees from the race course down the face of The Big Mountain, through rolling terrain to the bottom of what became Langley's Run, named for the President of the National Ski Association, Roger Langley.

That winter, Big Mountain instructors Toni Matt, Gene Gillis and Rhona Wurtele Gillis raced, having taken the winners' cups in the Doug Smith just a week before the Nationals.

On March 5 and 6, 1949, 80 male and 33 female racers converged upon Whitefish for the downhill, slalom and combined championships. A special edition of the *Whitefish Pilot* detailed ski events, noting that, "A die-hard load of skiers are going onto the hill early tomorrow morning to 'warm up the course,'" and suggested that the race course be named "'Schusser Slope,' but after the comments from the competing board artists, 'Suicide Sweep' might be more appropriate."

Advertisement in the 1949 National Championship program claims that these Flexible Flier Splitkein laminated skis are the "best in skis...designed to give you a full measure of fun."

Above: 1949 National Championships.
Right: a spectator pass and button from the event.

Crowded parking lot, 1949.

About 4,000 spectators watched the 1949 races, overflowing local lodging facilities.

"Everybody opened their home," said Arnold Hale, whose son Martin became so influenced by racing's greats that he would streak past the field of racers six years later to capture the Downhill, Slalom and Combined title — and tie for first in the cross-country section of the 1955 Junior Nationals!

"A couple of the years, we had two lovely young ladies, racers from the East, staying there at our home. Everybody did this. We served them breakfast and dinner, although sometimes they had dinner on the mountain. They were all good people."

Anxious to repeat the 1949 success, Winter Sports, Inc. again bid for national competition, and again hosted the Senior Championships in 1951, but this time, they were ready for the crowds. WSI had purchased the Northern Rocky Chalet from Ebb Schuehle for $25,000. The parking lot reportedly held 450 cars. Toni Matt and others cleared timber on the course. He and Russell Street spent hours peeling and painting saplings for the regulation-sized race gates, about two inches in diameter, strong and unforgiving enough to break skis and skiers in half.

Although dogged by a vicious blizzard that caused cancellation of some events, the 1951 Nationals drew 5,000 spectators to the slopes and big-name Olympians like slalom-winner Andrea Mead Lawrence.

The legacy of successful regional and national races and racers kept The Big Mountain in the news. As equipment and technique improved, so did clocked times. Where Savage's 65 mph topped races in the 1940s, by the 1990s, downhillers frequented speeds approaching 90 mph. Between equipment, clothing and race course design, skiers went through an evolution and a revolution. Leather boots and wool sweaters gave way to plastics, fiberglass, acrylics and synthetics. Course design became an art form. Coaching and racing became a profession.

Russell Street and Toni Matt painting racing gates for the nationals. They had to cut down saplings to get the hundreds of poles necessary for the big event.

Inclement weather during the 1951 nationals.

1948 map of The Big Mountain

Whitefish Ski Team in 1953 includes Buddy Babcock, Gordie DeVall, Glay Tallman, Toni Matt, John Seely, and Martin Hale.

Bidding for the Nationals

"Schenck and Prentice said, 'Why don't we send you to the national ski convention to bid for the national ski races,'" recalls George Savage who had helped build the Lodge and T-bar, and had won the 1941 high school state championship title. "So they bought me a coach ticket and put me on a train to St. Paul with no living expense money, just my $1.20-an-hour wage.

"All these people were there from Aspen and Mammoth to bid on the nationals. I thought, 'I got to do something and get a well-written letter to bid.' So I went to the hotel secretary and asked her to write a letter for me.

"I was pretty good at the cocktail parties and did a lot of lobbying with the different delegates. They awarded Big Mountain the nationals, I think because the delegates wanted to see this new and up-and-coming ski area. We beat out Aspen and Mammoth and Sun Valley."

If racing at the international level touched Flathead Valley skiers at all, it was protracted through successes of a handful of skiers who made national teams. After Martin Hale's debut as a Junior National Champion in 1955, Bill and Jim Barrier of the 1960 U.S. Olympic Team excelled in the '50s and '60s. Kalispell racer Jamie Lenon placed first in the Junior Nationals Downhill in 1966, and raced on the U.S. Development Team for three years with another local, Ken Patterson. Paula Kanerva won the combined senior women's title of North America in 1966. Tim Hinderman placed well in junior competitions, and collegiate championships in the early 1970s for the University of Colorado. Mike Porcarelli, four-time NCAA champion, raced on the U.S. Team in the 1960s,

The Woman Gets Results

In the midst of a pack of lycra and hard helmets stands Jessie Harring. She holds a felt pen in one hand and race results in the other.

For 25 years, Harring has been the band leader at the finish line: she strikes up a score and a cacaphony of hurrahs or mournful ahs follows. And for a quarter century, Harring has patiently suggested that the ski racers remember that these are unofficial results of the numerous downhills, giant slaloms, slaloms and now super Gs.

"Oh, I just enjoy the kids," says Harring, now in her '70s. "I got into the race officiating when my sons were ski racing, and I just kept going."

And keeps going. In 1950 she emigrated to Canada from Europe then to the states in '52, where she learned to ski in the Midwest before she and husband Don moved their family to Whitefish.

She volunteered on the Doug Smith Race in 1970. Officials took their places on the course. Harring remembers skiing down the outside of the downhill route because no one was allowed on the manicured course. She lacked strong skiing skills, and said it was a hair-raising experience just to get to the finish.

"It was bitter, bitter cold," she shivers, remembering the December morning. "We had old old chalk boards to write on with chalk. We tried to write names and results and everything was frozen. We had to put bare hands on the chalk board to melt the ice to write."

Part of the job of race official includes keeping the racers within the rules.

"If they swore, we were supposed to report them, which means disqualifying them," she says. "They come down angry, throw poles and swear. I just look at them. They say they are sorry. And I understand. When I started racing, I did the same thing. I was apprehensive. I've learned that because I did it myself."

That Harring not only skis but volunteers for the U.S. Forest Service amazes most people. After two hip replacements, not much slows her down. She races in local events (her favorite is the giant slalom) and wins in her age class, "because I'm the only one in my age class!"

Junior National Championships 1962, opening ceremony.

Planning the 1962 Junior National Ski Races in December 1961. Pictured left to right are Bill Martin, Bill Patterson, Swede Ormiston, Cal Jorgenson, James Mitchell, Bob Erickson, Jim Stephens, Howard Armstrong.

USA Moe-mentum

— FROM USA TODAY

followed by siblings Terri, Gail, and Tony Porcarelli on Junior National Teams in the 1970s. Brett Tallman and Alrick Hale found successes at the national level in the 1970s. Keith Veyna of Bigfork won the Junior Olympic downhill at twelve years old, raced on the World Junior Championship Team in 1984 and '85, and competed on the U.S. Ski Teams of 1988 and '89. Then Tommy Moe edged his way to an Olympic Gold Medal in the downhill and a silver in the Super G in 1994.

"I can still remember when I was three years old, skiing between my dad's legs on Chair Three on The Big Mountain," says Moe, the downhiller who honed his skiing edge on the North Bowl, now called Moe-Mentum. "Buck Love was one of my first coaches. I remember skiing with him, and he just let us ski. It was not structured, not regimented. We learned every run like the back of our hand."

Senior racers Nancy and Al Auseklis of Kalispell hold some 17 national and international Masters' Championship titles between them. Prior to moving to Kalispell, Nancy raced on the U.S. Ski Team in the early 1960s. *Ski Racing* magazine named Nancy "Outstanding Master" eight times. Six times she was named to the U.S. Masters' National Team, and was awarded the coveted "Al Sise Trophy" for

Keith Veyna wins the 1983 Doug Smith Downhill. Coach Kenny Manchester congratulates the champion.

Moe-Mentum sweeps The Big Mountain when Tommy Moe wins the 1994 Olympic Gold Medal in the Downhill in Lillehammer, Norway.

"My goal was to get in the top six and here I am with the gold around my neck."

Tommy Moe and his medals.

Left: Four members of the 1995-96-97 U.S. Snowboard Team are Flathead Valley snowboarders Tom Lyman, Steve Persons, Manuel Mendoza and Rob Berney.

Pure Air, Pure Water, Pure Fun

When one of the 1985 Ski/Yachting Championship contenders dove into the hot tub at race headquarters, (Kandahar Lodge) organizers Peter Brucato and Buck Love knew the first-ever event would become legend.

Carl Harper, a White Sulphur Springs cowboy whose ski gear predated the lifts on The Big Mountain, came up for air and bandaging.

"Carl Harper had to be taken to the hospital in an ambulance," recalls Buck Love. "The next day, bandaged and stitched up, he was ready to compete."

The venue listed two days of ski racing on The Big Mountain then two days of regatta on Flathead Lake. Skiing sailors from across North America brought ski boots and Top Siders to the Flathead Valley in hopes of winning the gold Rolex watch. The published venue did not include pre-race training. However, Harper's bloodied head became his hot tub handicap which helped him win the over 70 division.

"We started the event with competition in mind, and ended the event with new friends," recalls event organizer Heather Mull. "The overall most important thing we strived for in looking for a competitive event was that it had to be fun. We accomplished that."

The race committee decided upon The Big Mountain for its beauty and late-season snow, and upon Flathead Lake for its open water.

"We chose the site because Flathead is a beautiful high mountain lake that doesn't freeze over," says Mull. "And that year, the lake froze for the first time in 40 years! Luckily, just enough thawed to have the event. We joked about installing racing rules concerning what you do if you encounter an iceberg."

Give it wide berth!

Chilled Laser sailors warmed up in the hot tub after races in the 1985 event.

Above: Chilled laser racers Jeff Young, Ron Buldock and Greg Eaton in the first North American Ski Yachting Championships 1985, in hot tubs on the shore of Flathead Lake.

outstanding national competition, a trophy coincidentally named after her father.

"Team 'Fish,'" snowboarders Tom Lyman, Rob Berney, Manuel Mendoza and Steve Persons comprise a powerful force on the U.S. Snowboarding Team. Persons and Mendoza both tote World Cup gold medals from the 1995 and '96 seasons. Berney and Lyman scored podium finishes as well.

Telemark racer Neil Persons competed on the U.S. National Telemark Team in 1996 and won the Northwest Telemark Series and the Northwest Overall Championship in 1996. Another Big Mountain Telemarker, Chris Nelson, made the 1996 U.S. World Telemark Team.

For a relatively small community, the Flathead Valley produced a sizable number of outstanding racers, especially downhillers.

"We have a niche here," explains Brett Tallman, who now coaches youngsters. "We do well in downhills because we learn to ski soft snow. It takes a soft touch to be a good downhiller."

He adds that since The Big Mountain hosts downhill races every year, the racers tune skills on formidable terrain.

"Skiing in all conditions here makes us better skiers," adds Tallman. "We're not fair-weather skiers."

Race to the Place

"My husband, Jerry, and I are up on the mountain one day, and we hear about this race to town where they give out $100 to the first racer down before the cross country trail to town, the Race for the Place," recalls Kaye Groesbeck.

"It was 1978 and I didn't know the mountain very well but Gary Elliott assured me that the trail was well-marked. We start off at the top of the mountain, a mass start, a shot-gun start where everybody runs to their skis. I remember jumping over Tony Porcarelli because he fell or something.

"Well, the pack was far out of sight, so down to the bottom of Chair Four I skied. I'm the leader of the pack of women—me, Sally Porcarelli, Gaye Austin—about eight women total. Jeff Johns is near the exchange area where some people put on Nordic gear. He's waving us left down some trail. All the women follow me.

"At some point we realize we're on a lateral trek heading east to Columbia Falls. Whitefish is in the rearview mirror and the trail is getting gravelier and gravelier. And it's getting dark.

"Meanwhile, Betsy Honan, who was far behind us, arrived at the exchange at the lake, ready to quit the race. They tell her, 'No, don't quit. You're winning!' So she goes on the last leg and wins the women's race.

"Finally, about 6 p.m., the guys begin wondering where all the women are.

"By this time, we're somewhere near Columbia Falls, in the dark. All of a sudden, we see this white Suburban stuck in the snow and a guy trying to get it unstuck. We push him out and tell him he has to take us to The Place.

"We walk in just as the rescuers were about to go looking."

Above: Race to the Place competitor Dick Collins, 1972.

Far left: At the exchange station after the alpine section during the Race to the Place. The first skier to finish the alpine section snagged a $100 bill.

Left: Ski trails through the snowghosts.

Two Lawyers and a Casket

Frank Morrison, Gene Hedman and Terry Trombly won the Furniture Race to end all Furniture Races in 1974, after reaching nearly 60 miles per hour in their casket on skis. "We designed the casket with three Head Skis, a steering system and a brake," says Morrison. "I was steering, Gene was in the middle for ballast, and Terry was the brakeman.

"We got going pretty fast, and when Terry pulled up on the brake, it caught under the rail on the casket. He panicked and bailed out. There were probably 1,000 people at the bottom. I knew we were going to crash, so I steered to the right and hit a snow fence. I flew into the air and into a pickup truck in the parking lot. We won the race. Unfortunately a woman was severely injured by our casket. That was the last Furniture Race for a number of years."

Hungry Horse News columnist George Ostrom offered a limerick about the doomed cruiser:

There once was a sleek racing casket,

So fast that nothing got past it.

It came to a stop

in a large parking lot,

And the crew went home in a basket.

Crib on skis (above) and The Batmobile (below) competing in The Big Mountain's 1974 Furniture Race.

Coming through

A runaway coffin driven by Frank Morrison, Gene Hedman (middle) and Terry Trombly, crashed through the snow fence at the end of the raceway during the Frabert's Rainer Snowbust. The coffin hit a spectator and went into the parking lot area. The injured spectator was treated at the hospital and released. Morrison suffered three fractured ribs.

Ski racer in early race.

Patch from the Northern Division of the United States Ski Association.

'Top of Langlie Run' postcard by Lacy.

On Coaches and Coaching

Dry land training is to preseason ski fitness what cayenne is to cajun. Without it, an athlete won't have much of a ski season.

Dry land isn't new to the skiing frontier. Erik Rocksund, who ski raced on The Big Mountain in the 1960s, remembers that dry land training embraced endurance, strength and grit into a daily routine. Coach Jennings Cress pushed the racers to extremes.

"One of the things I recall about Cress was the workouts — they were tough. We used to run the power lines on what's now called Grouse Mountain," Rocksund recalls. "Or we'd run up The Big Mountain. Ski training was far more demanding than any training for football at Whitefish High School."

With Coach Cress, it was always a push for speed.

"We used to practice our downhill in his '59 Chevy four-door," says Rocksund, who is now a lawyer in Columbia Falls. "We'd drive Jennings' Chevy down Big Mountain Road using the snow banks like a toboggan run. The thing with Cress was always speed, and pushing corners as fast as we could. If there was a series of 'S' curves, you could cut out the corners, he'd say. So we did that. We used to drive like wildmen. And he was there to show us how to do it."

4

A Teaching Tradition

"We had come to Whitefish for three days and stayed for nearly nine years," recounts Stella Matt, wife of the famous Austrian ski racer, Anton "Toni" Matt, who ran the ski school on The Big Mountain from 1948 to 1956.

Upon invitation from Ed Schenck and George Prentice, the Matts stopped in Whitefish in the spring of 1948 after a trip to Banff, Alberta, where Toni acted for the ski film *Ski Pros Holiday*. Schenck and Prentice hoped Matt could replace Joe Ward, who ran the Karl Hinderman Ski School for The Big Mountain's inaugural year.

"We had received a letter from Whitefish asking Toni for his expertise in the planning of a ski run on The Big Mountain," says Stella. "I will never forget the reception we received when we arrived. Whitefish held the most hospitable people I had met."

Able to lure Matt away from Sun Valley, the fledgling ski area's supporters helped Matt open a ski shop. Stocked with some of the first production-line Head skis and Molitor and Henke boots, Toni Matt's ski shop and ski school opened with the falling of new snow.

"We thought Matt was really great," recalls Norm Constenius, "so we bought an eight-day lesson ticket — fifteen dollars. On the first day we had about a foot of new snow. I rode up the T-bar with Toni. Now, he was kind of an independent guy.

Opposite: Instructor Jim Black and skiing class amongst the snowghosts circa 1960.

Upper right: Ski School's bell.

Toni Matt 1920 - 1989

Toni Matt came to the United States in 1938, leaving his native Austrian Alps just one step ahead of the Nazis. He came to teach skiing for another Austrian, Hannes Schneider. The Arlberg ski technique of the legendary St. Anton ski school became the rage in Sun Valley. At 19 years old, Matt won the U.S. National Downhill Championship in 1939 and Combined Championship in 1941. George Prentice and Ed Schenck attracted Matt away from the star-studded Sun Valley by first asking him to design their new downhill race course.

The world-famous Matt was a coup for the young ski area in 1948. Equipped with a racing resumé longer than his 220 centimeter skis, Matt would be the drawing card that Schenck and Prentice needed. After all, Matt had shattered course records all over the states and in 1939, had challenged and won the "Inferno."

The Inferno, set on Tuckerman Ravine of New Hampshire's Mt. Washington, inspired fear in most skiers.

"I'd never seen a place that high and that steep," admitted Matt. "It looked like a cloud field." Those who challenged the frequently violent weather and steep face made turns. Many turns. But not Matt. An excerpt from *Esquire Magazine* tells it best:

"Other skiers in the 1939 Inferno raced down the sensible way, zig-zagging, not exceeding forty to fifty miles per hour. But Toni Matt, deciding to take it straight, rocketed down at sixty, then seventy, then eighty! Apparently losing control, he headed for a tree. But as cheers chilled the silence, he lunged, missed [the tree] by inches, flew across the finish line. Nobody had ever tried the Inferno since!"

Other headlines screamed, "Toni Matt, ski daredevil, admonishes imitators: Urges conditioning and technique before speed."

Opposite: Toni Matt summer skiing in Glacier National Park circa 1950.

1951-52 ski season brochure.

Toni Matt Ski School. Toni and wife Stella at right.

The St. Anton-am-Arlberg native instructed the top racing class at the Hannes Schneider Ski School, North Conway, New Hampshire. When the U.S. could take no more of the European thuggery and joined in World War II, Matt skied with the famous Tenth Mountain Division. At the war's end, he spent a year in Sun Valley's ski school with many other Austrian professionals.

After a junket to Banff, Alberta, to make the film *Ski Pro's Holiday*, Matt, with his bride Stella, stopped in Whitefish on invitation from Ed Schenck and George Prentice.

And on The Big Mountain he stayed, operating the Toni Matt Ski School and working the greens at Whitefish Lake Golf Course.

"We thought Toni Matt was really great," said Norm Constenius, retired Whitefish dentist. "He really laughed when anybody fell skiing. Like him, we'd go into peals of laughter when a guy would fall."

A half-day lesson cost $2.50, and private lessons $5.

Chapter 4 • *A Teaching Tradition* 43

In 1956, Matt's phenomenal racing career came to an abrupt end. Matt was persuaded to enter the famed Harriman Cup Race in Sun Valley.

"Toni was reluctant to go, and I had to let him even though I felt the same," recalled Stella, who stayed in Whitefish with their newborn, Carol, and their 3-year-old Marydeth. "When I received a phone call from Sun Valley the night before the race, Toni told me they were having a fresh snowfall. I knew this race was different. Never before had Toni called me before a race.

"The ski patrol did a fast grooming of the race trail. The visibility was poor, and Toni was going so fast he caught an edge and wound up in the trees where he was caught for hours before the ski patrol got to him.

"There were so many injuries that day. He waited all day for the doctor at the hospital to operate."

After months on crutches, Matt still limped and finally in 1956, friends brought Toni to New York City for a second leg operation. His ski shop was failing. The Big Mountain was still in financial crisis. Relatives invited the Matts to move to New England and start over. They remained in Pawling, New York, where Toni died in 1989.

Toni Matt circa 1950 in the powder.

Toni Matt, unknown skier, Jim 'Curly' Hitson and ski jumper Nils Hegvold circa 1953.

"When we got to the top and came down to the face of Hellroaring to wait for the other skiers, we waited and waited. Then Loren Kreck came up and obviously had fallen; then his wife, Mary, came and fell in front of us. Without saying a thing, Toni took off to the bottom. I said, 'Gee, Toni, aren't you going to give a lesson now?' He asked in his Austrian accent and renowned grin, 'How can I give a lesson if they can't even stand up?'"

They never did get their lessons, but received lots of instruction from Matt by emulating him.

"Toni had a real loud, piercing laugh," recalls Leona Constenius. "It was a very significant laugh and you could tell it was Toni from anywhere on the mountain."

In the Toni Matt era, skiing was Toni, and Toni was Austrian. The Arlberg technique, as taught across the nation, held that upper body rotation made the ski turn. Matt influenced many of The Big Mountain's best racers. Gary Tallman and Martin Hale kept up with Matt. Tallman eventually became the Montana Interscholastic Ski Champion. Hale captured the 1955 Combined Junior Nationals title. Matt began a legacy of highly respected ski schools on The Big Mountain.

Then a grave accident permanently sidelined the Austrian Adonis from aggressively skiing and racing. After a devastating fall in the Harriman Cup, Matt desperately needed surgery. With Stella and their children, Toni Matt regretfully left Whitefish in 1956 for New York where they remained.

Although Matt left a sizable impact on The Big Mountain, it was one of the early Hell-Roaring skiers who became the first certified ski instructor in Montana. Ole Dalen, who ventured onto the mountain in 1934, later served in the Army's Tenth Mountain Division. Before he fought in the Italian campaign where he lost his right hand, he skied and taught other soldiers to ski. He passed the instructor's examination on Mt. Hood, Oregon, in April 1940.

Karl Hinderman also served in the mountain corps. He opened the first ski school on The Big Mountain in 1947, but hired Joe Ward to teach while he taught in Sun Valley.

Hinderman returned in 1956 to run his own ski school. The French technique had come and gone; delayed shoulder, *wedeln*, and shortswing were popular for ski instruction only to die with the next round of successful European ski racers. On through reverse shoulder, counter-rotation, and the comma position, skiers lurched until Stein Eriksen's style took hold.

Peg Tully - Skier of the Day award. The award began in 1959 in the Karl Hinderman Ski School.

"I was Karl Hinderman's first instructor," says Dave Reitan, then a Minnesota farm boy of 19. "We came along with basically the Austrian technique, the reverse shoulder. Whoever scored well in the Olympics, then that country's style was popular."

During Hinderman's reign, American ski schools searched for an identity of their own, creating the Professional Ski Instructors of America in 1961 at The Big Mountain. Instructors from around the country arrived in Whitefish that spring to search for a higher level of professionalism, says Gerald Askevold, who joined PSIA that spring as the 131st member.

"PSIA formed because of divergent teaching methods in the U.S. versus recognized teaching methods in Europe," he says. "We were trying to establish a national identity in ski technique."

Scores of people learned to ski with the Karl Hinderman Ski School during the 16 years he ran the program. In those days, explains instructor Al Raddatz who began teaching in 1967, people came for the Ski Weeks and Ski Trains, and always took lessons.

"You didn't come to The Big Mountain unless you took lessons for three days, and most people extended for another two days," says Raddatz who still teaches skiing. "So guests skied hard for five days, and we really got to know them. Some people came back for ten or fifteen years," returning not just for the great skiing, but for the friendships they formed, explains Raddatz.

"Guests kept coming back because of the homey, no-glitz atmosphere," he adds. "Everybody ate together at noon. That was part of the American Plan package. We shut off Chair One for an hour. At one o'clock, they would fire up the chair, and everybody would go again. That ended in about 1973 because people decided to get modern and run the chair all the time."

Karl Hinderman 1916-1993

Karl Hinderman started the first ski school on The Big Mountain in 1947, although he hired Joe Ward to run the program that first year. After Toni Matt's era, Hinderman returned to his hometown of Whitefish from Sun Valley, where he'd taught skiing in the winters and guided fishing trips in the summers. The Karl Hinderman Ski School operated for sixteen years, until Karl retired in 1972. His wife, Nina, ran the Mountain Shop during those years.

The good-humored outdoorsman, who loved to fish and canoe, built into the ski school a solid program where guests would learn to ski in all conditions. But jumping was taboo for his three sons Toni, Tim and Jan.

"The thing I remember most about skiing and Dad was that we were absolutely forbidden to jump," says Tim Hinderman who was preschool age when the family moved up on The Big Mountain. "Kids love to jump. Any time we did jump, it was like breaking the law. One time I broke a pair of skis jumping, and I had to finish out the ski season on old skis that were far too short."

Hinderman's tenure was an era of radical change in teaching where techniques were modified every year. First the French technique, then Austrian, then American.

"Every fall we'd go out and decide which technique to teach that year," recalls Al Raddatz. "Finally the ski congress got together in Austria and decided on a unified technique called Inner Ski."

Other styles prevailed, but Hinderman's era marked an important time for skiing on The Big Mountain, a time when skiing grew to an international sport, and racing headlined the national news.

"Martin Hale and I were standing at the top of the Poma lift, going for an early morning get-together on technique with Karl," says Raddatz. "Karl came up behind us on the Poma. He lit a cigarette, and then zipped his coat up. When he got to the top, he found he had zipped his coat around the bar! Well, he couldn't get unzipped and the thing dragged him through the stop gate. We laughed and laughed. He laughed too."

Karl 'Dutch' Hinderman, Whitefish High School class of '35, was a nationally ranked skier and operated the ski school and shop in the 1960s and '70s.

Karl and Nina Hinderman at their ski shop.

'OK Coach,' titled photo by Lacy. Karl Hinderman and his son, Toni.

Karl Hinderman Ski School with the fifteen instructors.

Ski instructors Al Raddatz and Dave Reitan, 1980.

Although some of the intimacy was lost as the mountain grew, friendliness remained the single most attractive feature.

"We used to do demonstrations of ski school techniques for the guests," says Raddatz. "At noon hour, the instructors demonstrated the progression of skiing from snowplow to parallel turns. The tourists loved it, and we got to show off."

Meanwhile, Nina Hinderman operated the Mountain Shop.

"We had bought inventory from Toni Matt," recalls Nina. "There were some unedged skis and a few things. We sold Head skis, and we were the only shop between Spokane and Missoula with Heads. The only trouble was that we had to order eight pairs. 'Eight pairs!' said Ed Schenck, thinking of the prices, but the skis were sold before we even received them."

Those were the days when Willie Bogner introduced stretch pants at $55 a pair, and the shop presented weekly fashion shows to guests.

"Our main model was Eleanor Sneddon, who had modeled in San Francisco," Hinderman says. "She loved to ski and loved to model, and she had a pair of Bogners in every color."

At that time, the ski shop shared a tiny shack with the ski patrol.

"The only heat we had was a little pot-bellied stove," Hinderman says. "I set my cup of coffee on top of the stove, helped a customer, and when I came back, the coffee had ice on top."

The Hindermans later built the current ski shop building. Meanwhile, the success of local racer Martin Hale wasn't overlooked by Karl Hinderman. Hale became the head of the Hinderman Ski School and stayed there for thirteen years. Instructors Jim Black, Tom Moe, Sr. and Gary Tallman enlivened the teaching. Helmuth Matdies, another Austrian coach and instructor, thrilled the students.

"One time Dag Aabye was teaching a class, and Helmuth bailed over the whole class," says Raddatz. "Helmuth jumped over moguls and over the entire class!"

In 1972, Martin and Greta Hale officially opened the Martin Hale Big Mountain Ski School and Big Mountain Ski Shop. They doubled the square footage of the building, doubled the shop's inventory and by the 1990s, employed 80 instructors, sales clerks and rental shop personnel.

"Martin ran a clean, '60s kind of a school,'"

says instructor Donna Davis. "No cussing, no chewing, but most importantly, he did a lot of things for kids, always giving things away to kids so they could ski."

Hale offered a program to public schools that enabled children from as far away as Browning and Eureka to spend time on the mountain.

"Martin believed that there were too many kids in the valley that never ever got a taste of what the mountain was like, so he found a way for them to ski," says Nancy Hayes, Children's Ski School supervisor. "One year he brought Olney school up for nothing. The school was buying computers, so it didn't have money for skiing. Martin was very generous to kids."

The one thing Hale impressed upon his instructors was that kids should enjoy the mountain.

"Martin always said that it didn't matter if they ever learned anything," recalls former instructor Garry Jones. "They should just have fun."

Teaching styles came and went, evolving through the American Teaching Method then the American Teaching System with Martin's own adaptations. He maintained a staff with a seasonal return rate of 85 percent — one of the highest in the ski industry, according to instructor Linda Kuhlmann.

"Martin's approach to teaching skiing was to hire good people who he could make into fine instructors," adds Hayes.

Hale hired Bob Knauss, a superb skier known for the clowning around he did for his

Helmuth Matdies coached and taught skiing in the 1960s.

"I felt privileged to travel every weekend from Helena to Big Mountain to train with Helmuth Matdies," says Peggy Hollow-Phelps. "We'd tear up the Seeley-Swan in time to reach the mountain at 6:30 for night skiing on the 'whiz bang.' There were ten girls who skied with Helmuth. We bootpacked,...timed our mental runs and stayed out in below-zero weather. But we never learned how to yodel."

Gone Skiing

After a fresh snow, Ed Schenck would call up some regulars like dentists Norm Constenius and Loren Kreck.

"Many times from up on the mountain, Ed used to call me and say, 'Norm, gee there's some great powder up here. You'd better come up here,'" recalls Constenius. "Sometimes I'd call the afternoon patients and say, 'Do you mind if I go skiing this afternoon?' They'd always say 'no' and then I'd tell them to come in on Saturday."

One particularly powdery day, Constenius "dug himself into a big fishbowl," describes Kreck. "Now, the first thing you must understand about Norm Constenius, he doesn't like to put out money for anything. So I found his goggles and put them in my shirt. I told him he could buy some used ones at Karl Hinderman's Ski Shop."

Before the unsuspecting Constenius could get into the shop, Kreck went in and gave the goggles to Hinderman.

"When we stopped in the ski shop after skiing," says Constenius, "Karl said, 'Say Norm, I hear you couldn't find your goggles. I've got a slightly used pair here I'll sell you for a dollar.' I said, 'Yeah, I could use those. And I gave him my dollar."

"Norm's eyes popped out about a foot when he saw them," laughs Kreck. "Used. And a lot like the ones he'd lost!"

Constenius adds, "When I tried them on, I noticed they were wet on the inside. They all got a big laugh out of me for buying my old goggles back for a dollar."

Spademan Bindings

Working in the Rental/Repair Shop might not be the most glamorous position but employees made the most of sweat-tainted rental boots and P-Tex.

"Jerry Coffey, a ski instructor, skied on Spademan bindings, you know, the ones with no toe piece — we always gave him a hard time about those funny-looking bindings," says repair technician (and architect) Duie Millette. "So one time we took old toe pieces from some other bindings and glued them onto Jerry's skis. We cut screws apart and glued the screw heads on so it looked like we'd screwed them in."

Was Coffey upset?

"I was the guy they loved to give a bad time," says Coffey. "It was all in fun. They had a good time doing it."

After Coffey's bindings were doctored many times, Spademan finally went out of business and Coffey had to find another brand of bindings.

"Now they talk about taking the toe pieces *off* my skis," says Coffey.

While his skis have been spared as of late, his ski poles did not always escape unscathed.

"We slowly filled his ski poles with sand," admits fellow instructor Linda Kuhlmann. "We did it very slowly over days so he wouldn't notice. Pretty soon they had five pounds of sand in them, and he didn't notice. We had to hint and clue and joke to help him figure out that they were like lead."

Did Coffee deserve the pranks?

"Yeah," says Kuhlmann. "After all, he wore Spademans!"

classes, including climbing into old tree snags with his skis on. He hired Hoagy Carmichael, who told his female students to "keep all your abberdabbers pointed down the mountain." He hired Susan Schwarz, who got so involved in teaching small children the art of rope-tow riding that she forgot to put her own skis on when she went to ride the tow. And he hired Chyral Berney, a gem of an instructor who is afraid of heights.

"We practice lift evacuation to know what to do if the lift ever breaks down," says former instructor Anne Shaw Moran, now Executive Assistant at The Big Mountain. "I knew she was scared. Chyral and I got in line together, but Martin Hale grabbed Chyral to ride the lift."

In the chair in front of Hale and Berney sat Bob Knauss and Kenny Manchester. Both had practiced the evacuation procedure many times. First, a rope is thrown from the ground over the lift's cable. Attached to one end of the rope is a small chair or harness which is hoisted to the person on the lift. The person scoots onto the chair, and the people on the ground lower the person from the lift.

Gary Tallman and Maxine Williams ringing the ski school bell.

Instructor Ann Schwartz teaching Mark Williams, Maxine Williams and Jan Thrackmorten.

Martin Hale

"Martin was really getting into skiing," recalled his father, Arnold Hale, one of the early skiers who tirelessly volunteered on ski races from the first Doug Smith Memorial in 1948 until Arnold's death in 1996.

"For Christmas, we got Martin some ski boots," said Arnold. "Toni Matt came up and asked, 'What the hell you giving this boy a pair of slippers to ski in?' Toni bent 'em up and threw 'em into the stove. He gave Martin his very own pair of boots. That was the year Martin won the Junior Nationals and was invited to the Harriman Cup."

Growing up under the skiing shadow of world-great Toni Matt was for Martin Hale a priceless education. Born in 1937, Martin seized his father's excitement for skiing and Matt's flair for skiing fast.

"Martin was probably one of the sharpest guys of the young racers in knowing and understanding technique and what made a ski work," says ski instructor Al Raddatz. "He was a very good coach. His proteges — Tim Hinderman, Peri Schwartz, the Armstrong kids from Ronan, the Manchester kids, Gigi Braunberger — went far in skiing."

After Hale's successes in the 1950s, which took him across the country, he returned home to teach and coach for Karl Hinderman.

Headlines flashed "Martin Hale – Whitefish's only national ski champ."

"Martin was my mentor," says Tim Hinderman, currently General Manager at Schweitzer Ski Area. "He was a nut about physical conditioning, something that has stayed with me for life. His dry-land lessons stand out as much as the ones on snow. We'd be in the car for hours en route to races, and we'd learn lessons about defensive driving. He was a great influence on my life."

Hale did more than talk skiing to his students. He made customers into friends who returned for annual ski vacations for decades. He remembered customers' names even if once in a while he forgot names of his instructors, and gave everybody the middle name of "Lou."

"Martin always told us, 'Always treat people well,' and he believed that would make the ski school and the mountain better," recalls instructor Linda Kuhlmann.

His instructors describe Hale as shrewd, complex and a good "schmoozer," yet a mountain hero for what he did for kids.

"There was never a question that if a kid came up without enough money to ski, that Martin didn't find a way," says Hayes. "'We'll just slide 'em into a class,' Martin would say."

Not only did Hale affect thousands of customers in his 40-plus-year tenure, he helped crystallize friendships among his staff that have lasted well beyond ski season.

Martin Hale in untracked powder.

Inverted Instructor

"One of the funniest things I ever saw happened in 1974," recalls Reg MacDonald. "I ran the T-bar and was lift manager on The Big Mountain in those days.

"Jeff Fisher, a ski instructor, was over on the bunny slope teaching. When he was coaching, he would ski backwards. There was a spring under the snow, some eight feet down. Well, Jeff skied across that backwards, tipped over and his skis caught. He was stuck until they got somebody to rescue him!"

"It was a crazy thing," recounts Fisher. "Dick Peterson and I were teaching classes on the old T-bar which ran up a gully. I quite often skied backwards so I could talk to classes. Well, a creek had worn a big round hole under what's now Chair Three. Dick was riding up the Poma, and he watches me ski backwards, off the snow into a huge cavern. I stick one ski in one bank and the other ski in the other bank. Peterson laughed so hard that he fell off and got drug up the hill by the Poma. He finally got there and helped me just before I lost my strength. I went off backwards so I was leaning up against a wall over the top of swirling water, trying to keep from drowning."

"Kenny comes out first," says Berney, still shaken a decade later. "He goes upside down and flips over. He's done this a million times before. Then Bobby Knauss comes out, flipping and doing somersaults. I'm terrified. You have to let yourself slip off the chairlift and trust these two people on the ground with your life."

She finally eased herself out of the chair, thinking, "Hey, I'm with my boss here. I have to do this."

Then she grabbed Martin Hale's leg.

"I grabbed his boot and his leg. He's saying 'Chyral, let go.' I can't let go. He's kind of kicking me and saying, 'Let go.'"

Meanwhile, nearly the entire cast of ski schoolers watched from below.

"For twenty minutes she's hanging on to Martin's leg," says Kuhlmann. "We were all laughing hard. Finally she let go and was lowered to the ground safely."

"For a week after that," says Berney, "every time I'd see Martin, he'd start limping."

When he retired at the end of the 1994-95 ski season, Hale and his ski school were hardly limping along. Instructors taught 3,000 kids and 1,500 adults annually.

Skier John Davis in the snowghosts 1984.

As The Big Mountain turns the corner past its gold anniversary, it has taken over operation of the ski school. The staff has a combined 700 ski seasons of teaching experience. Several instructors have taught for more than twenty years. And 50 years after the first lessons in the Karl Hinderman Ski School, the 80 staff members combine skiing expertise with The Big Mountain tradition of friendliness.

5

Patrol: Iron Legs and Wooden Skis

Opposite: Patrollers Bud Eschwig and Gil Baldwin haul Dorothy Johnson in toboggan.

"Dorothy wanted to go to the top of the mountain that first or second year the mountain was open," recalls Marguerite Schenck. "So the patrol pulled her up on a toboggan. When they were coming down the hill, Ed [Schenck] happened to see the toboggan as he stepped out of the Lodge and said, 'Here comes the toboggan! This is no accident; it's Dorothy Johnson!' She laughed. She used that in many after-dinner speeches she gave as a famous writer of western stories."

Upper right: Ski Patrol patch from Whitefish Lake Ski Club.

By the late '30s, a few dozen skiers frequented the mountains above Whitefish on winter weekends. Laminated wood skis and rickety bindings demanded top performance from skiers.

Mully Muldown, Lyle Rutherford and Chuck Creon once again approached blacksmith Fred Hotel, who had created the Hell-Roaring Ski Club's rope tow. They had a plan for a metal binding to replace the leather straps that offered less stability than a flat-bottom boat in white water. Hotel welded together laterally rigid bindings.

"With these flanges fastened onto the boot or shoe, we were able to manipulate the ski a little better," said Mully. "A lot of times, the bindings caused injuries. In those days, nobody dreamed of a safety device. If a skier suffered a broken leg, we used a traction device made with his ski pole tied to the leg. People would say, 'Why didn't you bring him down on a toboggan?' Well, who was going to pull a toboggan up the mountain? It took a long time to get the injured person down, hobbling on the good leg, but at least he was involved in the rescue, free from hypothermia!"

"We had no formal patrol at that time," adds Lyle Rutherford. "Just that one skier would take care of another."

Not until after World War II did some of the Whitefish Lake Ski Club members organize a club ski patrol, and others organized the Satan's Mountaineers rescue group.

"We had to pass Red Cross certification classes in safety and winter first aid, and be an excellent skier," Otto Ost recounted. "We needed litter baskets to strap onto the toboggan, needed splints, and other gear for the patrol, so we raised funds to purchase equipment."

Even so, during the mountain's adolescent years, volunteer patrollers were recruited on the spot.

"When I broke my leg as a little kid, my neighbors brought me down in a toboggan," recalls Dale Evenson, who eventually became a pro-patroller and mountain manager in the 1960s.

By the time The Big Mountain bid for the 1949 nationals, local druggist Bob Haines offered to teach the first Red Cross class for ski patrol. During the nationals, ski clubs from around the country brought their own ski patrols.

"We had lots of good help," says Rutherford, who had taken that first Red Cross class. "We stationed them all over the mountain with toboggans. And we used them."

The mountain dedicated a room in the lower Ski Lodge for patrol work, then later, Dr. John B. Simons offered to pay for a patrol shack.

"Schenck drew up a design for the patrol shack, and volunteers built it," says Rutherford. "It had a bunk bed or two and a stove. It sat just left of the Lodge."

Patrollers and toboggans skidded into service. They planted skis into the snow, crossed the skis' tips and thus marked "caution: injured skiers."

Part of the ski patrol job on The Big Mountain included grooming the slopes.

Satan's Mountaineers rescue group as pictured in the 1949 National Championship program, which states: "Satan's Mountaineers, a group of local skiers, both men and women, was organized to form an efficient and versatile rescue group." The group includes Betty Kell Nucci, Otto Ost, Marge & Ernest "Tap" Tapley, Bob Overman and Cleo & Gil Baldwin.

"We formed Satan's Mountaineers to learn skiing in dangerous areas — roped together while on skis — and to learn rock climbing," recalls Betty Nucci. "We were only together as a group for a little over a year."

"We ski-packed the run down the T-bar where Chair Two is today," recalls Stuart Swenson, who ski patrolled in 1959. "People were on long wood skis, 210 to 215 centimeters, and couldn't ski powder. We made two passes side-stepping down the slope in the morning and two passes down in the afternoon."

While more and more skiers enjoyed

First Casualty

The National Ski Patrol was in its infancy, having just formed in 1936, after a couple of tragic ski accidents in the East focused on a need for an organized battalion of patrollers nationwide. At the Hell-Roaring Ski Club, an injury meant a long adventure into town.

Lyle Rutherford won the grand distinction of being the first serious causality of Hell-Roaring Ski Club members during the winter of 1938-39.

"We were up at the top of the mountain where the upper terminal is now," recalled Rutherford. "It was just a bad day. We had breakable crust, flat light, and I was skiing too fast when I started a big turn."

"I caught the crust a couple times," said Rutherford. "I went end over end and I heard a crack. It was my right leg just above my ankle. We had no ski patrol, so I skied down on one ski. I caught it a couple more times and had to sit down and wipe my face off with snow to keep from passing out. It was quite painful."

Luckily for Rutherford, Dr. James Brown happened to be on the mountain that day. Brown stabilized Rutherford for the long ride to the hospital. The skiers made a make-shift sled from Rutherford's skis, nailing the skis together. Before taking him to town, friends had a chance to snap a photo of the victim.

Funeral for injured skier, Lyle Rutherford, who didn't really die, just broke his leg. "Somebody got the old climbers' register and held it open like a Bible and read over me," laughs Rutherford. Others in the 1938 photograph include Betty Muldown, Bill Kammar, Bud Dalen, Ole Dalen, Tom Dempsey and Jo Measure.

COURTESY CHUCK CREON

Lyle Rutherford circa 1950. COURTESY LYLE RUTHERFORD

"Those meatheads!" laughs Rutherford, "They were acting like it was my funeral," he says of the photograph.

After a lengthy slide down the mountain, Al Taylor met them with a four-horse team pulling a sleigh for the ride from near where Ptarmigan Village is today, on into Whitefish. Rutherford's leg was properly set at the tiny hospital, and Rutherford vowed to become a part of a national movement to train skiers in first aid.

First grooming mechanism, the slat roller.

The Big Mountain, moguls sprouted like dandelions on a lawn.

"We had to go out and shovel the moguls," continues Swenson. "George and Bill Murphy and I thought, 'There must be a better way.' So we got some dynamite. Well, we gave it our best shot. It didn't work. We blew a big hole in the slope."

Eventually grooming equipment roamed onto slopes. The first roller and mogul cutter rolled behind the Tucker SnoCat over fresh snow and packed it down. It didn't work too well.

"Dale Evenson, the patrol leader, hired me to shovel moguls in 1965," says Bob "Moke" Muraoka, who eventually worked his way onto ski patrol and served as patrol leader in '79 and '80. "I'd ride the chair up every morning and shovel all day. It was something that had to be done. I just used a big snow shovel. Moguls in those days were huge deep moguls — long football-shaped things."

Despite the advent of sophisticated grooming machines, patrollers still packed shovels and did hand work as needed. Yet patrolling wasn't all work and no play. Swenson remembers at the end of the day when the team of patrollers headed by George Murphy schussed the T-bar line after the lift closed.

"We always ended up turning, but we had some wild trips down the T-bar line," he says.

In 1960, with the installation of the Chair One to the top, The Big Mountain Pro Patrol formed. Cal Tassinari headed the inaugural pro patrol of five men.

"It became a formal organization with Red Cross credentials, first aid, avalanche training and lift evacuation training," says Tassinari who became Hill Manager in 1961. "Each year we became more and more professional."

Using crude tools, patrollers were heroes.

"I walked into the patrol hut at lunchtime one day, and a patrolman was cutting a piece of plywood," recalls Tassinari. "We used to cut plywood to make leg splints. 'Can't you do that after lunch?' I asked the

1975 Ski Patrol bash on the deck of the Bierstube. Some partygoers are Bob Muraoka, Dick Peppoel, Mike Muldown, Guy Ridenour and Beth Ridenour, Karla, Jan Metzmaker, Jim Hietel, Denny Rea, Mark Salisbury, Tom Eisenger, Bill Kline. Beginning of a tradition, on the last day of the season.

guy. He answered, 'No, there's a guy up there with a broken leg, and I need to make a splint.'"

Portable radios were not available to the patrol, yet patrolmen did their job well. Until the 1970s, the North Bowl and Haskill's Slide remained out of bounds. Avalanche danger ran high. Tassinari and another skier were partially buried in a slide but escaped with only broken skis.

"We thought of ourselves, not as suave as the instructors, but amongst the very capable skiers," adds Tassinari. "We were called 'Iron legs on wooden skis.' We usually knew half the people skiing by name, and we were encouraged by Ed Schenck to eat lunch with the guests. It was a very informal, congenial era of The Big Mountain."

Postcard by Ed Gilliland of skier Gary Bennett, former patroller.
"Snowghosts on The Big Mountain add beauty as well as a challenge to the slopes."

Ski patrol name badges.

Through Patrol Directors Dale Evenson, Joe Muretta, Gene Evans and Steve Spencer, the ski patrol grew.

"We had lots of good times but we didn't do crazy things," says Evenson. "We were pioneers in patrolling. A busy day meant 80 skiers. We invented devices that are now mandatory, like a safety back-up brake on lifts and lift evacuation training. We used a plain old wooden toboggan. We got Bob Anderson of Gull Boats in Missoula to make up a fiberglass toboggan."

They thought of themselves as professionals and worked out challenges masterfully. Even skiing challenges met a match in Evenson, who placed cardboard or magazines on his shins above ski boots to ski rain-crusted snow. They skied in it all.

"We'd ski down the real steep stuff on Haskill's Slide," recalls Ed Gilliland, who patrolled in 1964 and '65. "The one thing I used to hate to do was pack moguls out with skis, shovel them in and pack with skis. It was hard work. Then somebody — usually

Evenson — would yell, 'No alibis,' and that meant you raced to the bottom, straight down over non-groomed bumps."

That was all part of an unspoken code that said, "If you can't ski it, stay out of it," according to Mike Muldown who patrolled in the early 1970s. "We had somewhat of a rite of passage for new patrolmen. The other patrollers harassed you to get into stuff you didn't want to get into. It meant drinking beer every night until the Bierstube closed then getting up and skiing the worst of wind slab the next morning."

Breaking the code meant a Frabert Award, as Muldown found out.

Dale Evenson, ski patrol director, holding the December 1963 SPORTS ILLUSTRATED that featured Jim Black skiing The Big Mountain. The article said that The Big Mountain's 'real appeal is the aura of friendliness.'

"I was working Chair One with Cliff Persons one miserable day," he recalls. "The skiing and visibility were so bad that it took Cliff, a really great skier, 25 minutes to ski from the top of Chair One to I.S., the intermediate station. It took me 40 minutes. Gropple built up on your glasses. You couldn't see or ski. So when it came time to go down for lunch, instead of skiing down, I jumped on the lift to I.S., then skied down from there."

Word spread across the mountain like a poison oak rash.

"Everybody averted their eyes when I'd come along," laughs Muldown. "When I went to get back on the chair, the lift operator looked away from me like he was thinking, 'You broke the code.'" Awarded a Frabert, Muldown had to drink a "yard of beer," from a three-foot long mug.

"I had the greatest times of my life there because I was young, because it was a hell of a challenge, and it was something I truly loved then and now," Dale Evenson adds. "I always said when I died, I want my ashes put up there by the statue of Jesus."

The trail map and Snow Ranger John Hauer with Tom Moe, Sr., 1959-60.

Opposite: Cal Tassinari in deep snow, early 1960s.

"We spent the day in the Drift area," recalls Tassinari of the day Marion Lacy made this photograph. "It was a critical thing to get the turn where Marion wanted it. I went along skiing with Marion because he had broken his leg a few years before, and he needed a skier who could pack his camera. We had a lovely day but at the end, I had his equipment while we skied down, and Marion fell and broke his leg again."

The Bierstube

From the earliest December days on The Big Mountain, the Ski Lodge walls shook and rattled to the quake of dancing ski boots. The Stube, as it's affectionately known, opened in the old Lodge which was located at the north end of the present Moguls' site.

"It was quite a social scene," recalls Stuart Swenson, who was on ski patrol in the late 1950s and later joined the ski school. "When you got through with a can of beer, you'd throw it up into the rafters. There were hundreds of cans up there."

Somebody had to clean out the rafters come spring.

"The odor from the supply of months of old beer cans ... was so foul that the operation could only be carried out long after the ski season ended," remembers Norm Kurtz, chief can cleaner. "Ed Schenck assigned the cleaning job to me early one spring. I parked a dump truck under the eaves of the Bierstube, where I pulled off the underside boards of the overhanging roof to allow the beer cans to drop into the truck. I've never been capable of drinking more than an occasional beer since!"

Others did partake and on particularly busy nights, while Ed Schenck served the suds, beer sloshed onto the wooden floor and dripped into a room below.

Skiers perched on the open rafters where they learned the fine art of drinking while hanging upside down, "defying both gravity and digestive sensibility," says Kurtz.

Aprés ski in the original Bierstube with Nils Hegvold and Jeanne Tallman.

On October 31, 1963, a fire burned the Stube, including the original Frabert monkey, and much of the original Lodge. In 1966, instructor Jim Black and his wife, Joyce, hired Gary Tallman to build a new Bierstube. Decorating the exterior of the building were painted signs of Bavarian skiers in red jackets and black pants. Inside, customers could buy charcoal steaks and sandwiches, and sit at tables surrounding the wood dance floor.

When they opened the Stube that winter, the Blacks raised the price of a beer to 35 cents for a mug and 40 cents for a red beer.

"People were upset," recalls Joyce (Black) Swenson. "Beer had been a quarter for a mug."

The Blacks managed the business for five years before selling it to The Big Mountain.

"It used to be kind of rowdy," recalls ski instructor Al Raddatz. "Well, one night, things were pretty slow, so we took an old pair of Kazama skis, opened doors on both sides of the Stube, and got up on the ski hill side of the parking lot. We jumped into a tuck and skied across the parking lot and through the Stube."

The skier then grabbed a rope that hung from the ceiling to swing on through the back door and off the end of the deck.

"In those days, there was not hardly a drop off the back because there was no lower parking lot," chuckles Raddatz. "Ed Schenck put a stop to it. We were getting a little carried away. He had a twinkle in his eye when he said don't do it anymore."

The Stube may have been fun, but it was failing financially. Meanwhile, a bar owner in town named Gary Elliott mouthed-off that "If I ran the Stube, things would be better," recalls Elliott. "One day this guy, Norm Kurtz, comes in to my bar and says, 'I hear you think you can run the Stube.' So I leased the Bierstube in 1972. It was a third of the size it is now."

After that first year, Elliott says, he had to agree to another year's lease because he hadn't made enough money to cover the first lease! Since then, Elliott and WSI expanded the building and the deck, and the business. He annually buys ten tons of hamburger for Back-door Burgers, and packs a few hundred ski-boot stomping guests into the Stube for bands like Asleep at the Wheel, Bo Didley, Elvin Bishop, Vassar Clemments, The Drifters, The Boxtops and The Beat Farmers.

"Skiing in itself is not even half of visitors' experience," says Elliott. "They may spend four or five hours skiing. We at the Bierstube concentrate on the activities and experiences for the off-slope time, things that give them something to talk about aside from skiing when they get home."

Kurtz agrees. "A lot of folks have said the growth in popularity of The Big Mountain as a place to ski among Canadian skiers should be rated equally among The Big Mountain, Moose's Saloon and the Bierstube," says Kurtz. From early on, "the skiing day ended with a crawl upstairs into the original Lodge at the Bierstube."

After the Punk Rock Nights, the Waitress Cups, and the Upside-Down Beer Drinking contests, the Stube remains neighborly; all newcomers are given a Bierstube ring in silver or gold, free for the asking.

Stube Crew 1984 includes (front row) Eric Streich, Curt Goble, R.D. Giesy, Don McConnel, Tom Hilley, Buddy Flint, (back row) Barry Smith, Gary Elliott, Bert Riley, Jim Goble, Jeff Johns, Pat Frerich and Kerry Crittenden.

Patrollers came and went but it wasn't until Patrol Director Steve Spencer broke boundaries in the winter of 1975 that women joined the pros' ranks.

"I didn't intentionally become the first woman ski patroller on The Big Mountain," says Terri Rolseth Montgomery, a registered nurse who felt her medical skills could help the patrol. She didn't fit the macho mold nor did she fit the huge, worn-out red jacket. "I had a hard time because some guys were angry that I broke into the 'all-boys' club.' It was sacred territory for some. I remember that Peggy Spencer—trying to make things easier on me—said to her husband Steve, the hill manager, 'It's kind of like pets, Steve. If you have one, you have to have two.' So he hired Linda Lee Kanzler a few months later."

"It was a new and big step for the mountain to hire women for patrol," admits Chris Bowman, who was hired a year later. "It really started the winter before, when I was hired to work on lifts. I was under a microscope then, so sliding onto patrol was pretty easy. It certainly wasn't considered women's work in those days."

"By the end of the year, the guy who gave me the hardest time finally admitted that he was reluctant when Spencer hired a woman," says Montgomery, who went back to a nursing career. "He told me that I did toe the line."

Chapter 5 • *Patrol: Iron Legs and Wooden Skis*   61

Frabert's Follies

The weekly "Frabert" award, given out Wednesdays at the Bierstube, dates back to about 1960. The three-foot tall stuffed toy monkey, mascot to the ski patrol, headlined the clod-of-the-week award.

The name "Frabert" came from patrolman Stuart Swenson's college days when he visited "a derelict from Billings with the first name of Frabert."

"Frabert was given out as an award by the patrol on kind of a daily basis in the beginning, to the clod of the day for some foolish stuff seen by somebody," says Tom Unger, who ski patrolled and was Mountain Manager in the 1960s. "When everybody got together in the Bierstube after skiing, the clod got to come up and accept the award with a mug of beer to chug-a-lug."

A patrolman, often Unger or more recently, John Gray, recited the Frabert Follies poem to the award winner: "Here's to the skier who skis so fast, who leaps over moguls and falls on his ass!"

The original Frabert burned in the 1963 Ski Lodge fire. The patrol quickly replaced the lost monkey with the current version, and a local physician doctored up the leg cast.

One of the classic Frabert's Follies, says John Gray, occurred when two Delta airline pilots flew into Kalispell for a few days off.

"Do you ever wonder why your luggage doesn't go where you go?" asks Gray. "It seems no one was there at the airport to meet the pilots. They called The Big Mountain, 'What's going on?' Well, Big Mountain Reservations looked it up and found that the pilots were to go to Big Sky for their days off! Reservations called me so we set them up. When they came down to the Stube, of course they received the Frabert — a real crowd pleaser. The mountain put them up for the week and they had a great time."

Frabert and friend, David Hartman, national television show host. Hartman was Grand Marshall for Winter Carnival 1971.

COURTESY GARY ELLIOTT

One of the all-time biggest Fraberts led to a ski patrol golden rule of sorts. As the story goes, a few years ago, a young guy wanted to work for the patrol.

"It was the classic 'Cool Winter' ski movie story of a young guy working in the Ptarmigan Room restaurant who wants to get on patrol," says Patrol Leader Chet Powell. "A patroller gets injured so we need to hire. He's working Chair Two and this is back in the days of few radios. He was led astray by another patroller, and they skied off the backside, outside the boundary to get powder. The new guy didn't know the cut-back trail in bounds. At the same time, there were two accidents on Chair Two and when he was called on the radio to respond, he couldn't because he had gone too low and was on his way to the lake."

Other patrollers responded to the injured skiers while the young patroller slogged out of the woods and hitchhiked back up the mountain.

"What made things worse was his denial that he got lost," says Powell. "When we asked what happened, he said his pipes had broken and he had to leave to fix it! We wondered why he took his skis and left his truck on the mountain. Major Frabert for that!"

The Bierstube

COURTESY THE BIG MOUNTAIN

Riding Down the Chair

Sometimes riding the chairlift is a bit of a challenge as Bob "Moke" Muraoka discovered in 1977.

"I was working on patrol early one morning," he recalls. He'd gone to the top of Chair One to shovel the ramp when an empty chair nearly knocked him off the ramp, a considerable drop of more than 20 feet. He caught himself from falling by grabbing the back of the chairlift seat.

"After I realized it was a far drop, I thought I could get into the chair," says Moke. Hampered by heavy ski boots, he couldn't quite pull himself into the chair. He dangled a hundred feet and more as the chair approached the lip of Ptarmigan Bowl.

"I was finally able to swing myself partially into the chair, and wedge my stomach onto the side of the chair," laughs Moke. "It was hard on my stomach. There was no one at midway because it was too early in morning."

But someone else rode the chair.

"I was taking a fun run on Chair One first thing one foggy morning," recalls Al Raddatz. "I was on the chair, about half way up the face when I hear this voice hollering,

Bob Muraoka, Donny Hall and Steve Spencer circa 1975.

and I see somebody dangling from a chair, coming down. It was Moke! Funniest sight I'd ever seen, coming on in the quiet morning with somebody hollering through the fog."

Moke bailed off at the Intermediate Station unscathed, assured that the entire mountain would hear of his mishap. He couldn't avoid a Frabert Award.

Ski Patrol during avalanche training circa 1961.

Ski patrol cross with the ptarmigans and mountain insignia. The idea behind the ptarmigan, says patroller John Gray, was the summer/winter resort, changing your feathers. "Now we have the billy goat on the coats."

Big Mountain Ski Patrol circa 1985.

Chapter 5 • Patrol: Iron Legs and Wooden Skis

Regardless of the extra large coats, the off-color jokes and a shared locker room where long johns were the *vetements du jour*, they had fun.

"I was a boiler-plate skier from Minnesota," laughs Montgomery. "In mashed potatoes I was in trouble. They had this fall chart and you paid ten cents for every fall. I think I owed money by the end of the year. Anyway, I supplied the beer for the party that year with all my falls."

By the mid 1990s, under the direction of patrol leaders Chet Powell and John Gray, the staff grew to 23 patrollers to accommodate the nearly 300,000 skiers annually cruising the crushed-velvet grooming or charging through fresh Rocky Mountain powder. As ski gear and grooming improved, the work transformed from splinting legs and boot-packing runs to speed and safety management.

Every afternoon when the lifts stopped rolling, the patrol and ski school did "sweep" – a scan of the runs for pokey skiers. Often they'd flush out a couple of grouse and a Mully Muldown, who liked to observe skiers from the quiet woods. The last patroller, the "Super Sweep," tucked Toni Matt Run and raced to the Patrol Hut at the bottom. Neil Persons' 1990 schuss remains in the Ski Patrol Record Book at one minute, 47 seconds. The race begins on the telephone and ends after the patroller removes skis, crosses the parking lot and runs up the patrol room stairs.

"After the other patrollers made sure all skiers were off the mountain, they called me at the top and called, 'Clear!'" recalls Persons, who wore his helmet and 212 centimeter skis. "As soon as I hung up the phone, they started the timer. I had to lock the windows and door, put on my skis and tuck Toni Matt at the end of the day when small moguls look huge at 80 miles per hour."

Despite madcap events, or in spite of them, to the public the ski patrol, in flashing-red jackets with white crosses, maintains an air of dignity and professionalism. When the coats came off, it was beer drinking, leg wrestling and Spencer riding his motorcycle through the Bierstube. And, of course, the endless pranks.

Front page of the Whitefish Pilot, January 25, 1979. Danny On died in a ski mishap at the age of 55. The Danny On Trail on The Big Mountain is dedicated to his memory. On was a Forest Service silviculturist, renowned nature photographer, conservationist, and avid skier.

Patrolman Randy Gayner owned a pair of white Scott ski boots. "Everybody decided that a patroller did not wear white ski boots," says Assistant Patrol Leader, John Gray.

"So we painted them. Brown."

Over the past half-century, The Big Mountain Patrol has successfully aided thousands of injured, lost or just plain scared skiers, due primarily to the professionalism of patrol brigades who keep the dangerous areas posted and search all night, if necessary, for lost skiers. Volunteers from the Flathead Valley Nordic Patrol, North Valley Search and Rescue, and Flathead County Search and Rescue team up for searches out of the ski area boundaries.

Ongoing training attunes the staff to the intricacies of first aid in a changing industry. Where Mully and the Hell-Roaring skiers treated broken legs, the advent of safety bindings, groomed slopes and snowboarding means the patrollers more often see knee and joint injuries. According to Patrol Leader Chet Powell, typically 1.9 skiers per thousand need patrol assistance on The Big Mountain, lower than the national average of 3.4 per thousand.

"Patrolling is an ever-changing, always interesting responsibility," says Powell. "It's not only the great and diverse personalities of the group but the new challenges of the mountain's added terrain that keep the patrol job rewarding. The biggest reward for patrollers comes in helping people, offering words of advice, directions or just a friendly hello."

Above: Crazy ski patroller Mark Bloomquist, Halloween 1985. Top center: Ski patroller and skiing clown, Steve Klaas, dressed up for Special Olympics. Klaas later died of an aneurysm while skiing his favorite run, Good Medicine. At right: Ski patrol Randy Gayner digging a snow pit, checking snow depth.

6

Beargrass & Huckleberries

Once snows finally gave way to beargrass, Indian paintbrush and wild rose, the Whitefish Range awoke. The mountain's "forest values" were described in a 1913 U.S. Forest Service report as having "high timber value. This forest unit has been so inaccessible that it has had little use in the past outside of hunting and trapping, which have been carried on for the past 15 years. The trails which the hunters use are snowshoe trails and are impassable during the summer."

Early records date wildfires of 1910 and 1919 that swept away decades of underbrush and timber, creating natural ski runs for Muldown, Dalen and the Hell-Roaring bunch. According to U.S. Forest Service documents, "The 1910 wind-driven fire in Hellroaring drainage burned about 2,500 acres. That fire started in the valley bottom near Whitefish Lake and burned to the top of Whitefish Divide."

The other large fire began in Haskill Basin during the summer of 1919, burning 2,000 acres from valley bottom to ridge top. Since then, some 50 smaller fires licked at the timber, but no significant amount of acreage has burned.

Before World War One, Ichinojo Sakarai, a native of Hatsubara, Japan, ran a trapline along the Whitefish Divide and lived in a cabin on The Big Mountain. A few irascible miners claimed valuable ore on the mountain's

Opposite: Summer over snow. Randy Schmechel and Doreen Ibsen riding old Chair One.

Upper right: Postcard of Summer on The Big Mountain by Lacy.

shoulders, and of course Whitey Henderson dug lime from the lower mountain.

In the 1930s and '40s, summer visitors grazed the slopes, drank from the streams and fertilized the soil. The Polson Grazing Company drove a herd of sheep over stage roads, through downtown Whitefish, along the lake and up to summer pasture.

Huckleberries drew bears and berry pickers into the beargrass and kinnikinick. Otto Ost recalled picking huckleberries and selling them for 50 cents a gallon in the late '30s.

Whitey Henderson tried charging a few nickels to guide pickers to bountiful berries, Mully Muldown recalled, although Mully refused to pay for the scouting.

The skiers used Henderson's trails to find their cabins until 1939 when the Forest Service built a six-mile road up the mountain. The Forest Service improved the road in 1947 with $15,000 and plenty of volunteer labor.

"My dad would go up and work weekends widening the road," recalls Charles Abell. "There were no chain saws, mostly hand saws called 'Swede fiddles.' I'd be the water boy."

Somebody soon figured out that the upcoming election meant a "real reservoir of manpower," Ed Schenck said to *The Saturday Evening Post*. "[W]e got on the phone and called all the candidates in the county and invited them to labor with us. It was just as mandatory for politicians as an invitation to a church social. By the time the road was finished, the Forest Service figured that more than $5,000 in work had been contributed."

Once Schenck and George Prentice's vision of The Big Mountain began, summer became a scramble of construction, installation, renovation, restoration and recreation — a continual renaissance to avenge winter's harshest weather and mend scars from ski boots. First Schenck and Prentice hired a crew to clear a 600-foot swath for the T-bar and to

Clearing the Langley run for the 1949 Nationals. Toni Matt chops down a tree with ax. Others in photo include Mully Muldown, Chuck Creon, Russ Street, Gub Akey and Ole Dalen.

'Adjacent to the huge one and one-quarter mile double chairlift is 'Alpinsnack' where visitors can enjoy light lunches while watching 'lunker' trout swimming in the clear waters of the resort's rearing pond.'

build the Ski Lodge. While Whitefish's population held at 2,600 in 1947, not all the residents thought a ski area could survive.

Detractors emphatically said that WSI stock's worth fell somewhere between rocks and pebbles. Yet Rusty Abell, president of Whitefish Credit Union, and Shirley Lincoln, owner of Lincoln's Cleaners, sold stock until even the mountain's milk bill was paid.

"The detractors did not have any vision beyond tiny Whitefish," says Jane Seely Solberg. Her father, Brad Seely, Chamber of Commerce President in 1947, backed WSI and was second in line to purchase WSI stock. "Some people back then said that we must concentrate on making Whitefish a summer resort and support the downtown businesses instead of some wild dream on a mountain top."

In 1952, Schenck began keeping records on the number of summer visitors. Twelve-thousand people made the muddy trek up the mountain to ride the "scenic chair," a single-seater with a plywood seat on an S-shaped bar that dangled from the T-bar cable.

After 1961, summer passengers rode Chair One to the top of The Big Mountain. The views of Glacier National Park and the Canadian Rockies exceeded expectations.

When the old Chair One was replaced with a high-speed quad chair and gondola cars in 1989, sightseeing expanded to dinners and conventions in the Summit House, winter and summer. At its gold anniversary, over 50,000 summer visitors trek along the slopes on The Big Mountain, many of whom hike the four-mile Danny On Trail through larch and Douglas fir, sub-alpine terrain and scrubby fir of treeline at the top.

In 1950, Sverre and Katherine Askevold bought the first lot sold by WSI for the equivalent of a week's stay in a condo at 1997 prices. Katherine recalls making the deal over a cup of coffee with Schenck. WSI had purchased "360 acres in 1947 for a dollar an acre!" adds Marguerite Schenck. The Askevolds built a cabin that summer, and by the late 1950s, a handful of cabins and homes dotted the area.

Few people stayed year-round on The Big Mountain. Nina Hinderman, who owned and operated the Mountain Shop, recalls that she and Karl bought a house from Harley Hartson for $7,500 in 1956, and lived on the mountain with their three young sons. During the summer of 1959, they had bear trouble.

"We had a big dog that stayed mostly outside," recalls Nina. "We'd put food out for the dog, but a black bear would get to the food first. I always knew when the bear was around because the dog would run inside and get under a bed."

First residence on The Big Mountain built by Sverre Askevold.

Chapter 6 • *Beargrass & Huckleberries* 69

Original Hell-Roaring Ski Club rope tow and the high-speed quad, Glacier Chaser.

The Big Mountain summer theater, 1963 Mountain Playhouse of "Night Must Fall," includes Ann McKenna, Anne Klein, Nancy Nei, Richard Klein, Wandalie Henshaw, Wendy Wallace, and John McKenna.

> ## Bear Sightings
>
> "We have a sign that says 'Please report any bear sightings,'" says Elaine White, Ticket Manager on the mountain. "This lady had seen our sign and came to tell us all about the bear she'd seen. 'I'm just sure it was a griz,' she said, all excited about it. We asked her where she saw the bear. 'I backed my car up next to it,' she told us. I thought, 'Wow, we've got a bear in the parking lot!' So we asked her exactly where she parked her car. 'Well, at Logan Pass,' she answered."

Karl had tired of the thievery one day and grabbed his gun.

"Bears were a backyard phenomenon," says Tim Hinderman. "Dad shot the bear out of a tree. I remember that blood splattered all over the clothes on the clothesline. I think Dad was in trouble for that."

"I had a clothesline full of clean white clothes," laughs Nina. "At the time, I didn't want to wash them [by hand] all over again."

Hibernating bears emerged from dens on the mountain, sometimes before the end of the ski season. A few grizzly bears staked claim to slope-side huckleberry crops, but no bear has evoked such wonder as the griz that perfected his backstroke on the mountain in 1995.

The Big Mountain had dredged a holding pond, the Upper Reservoir, for snow-making purposes. Placed on the upper mountain between the Big Drift and Toni Matt runs, the pond attracted some wildlife, but one September day in 1995, people spotted a griz swimming in the pond.

Garth Weaver, who operates the Old West Adventures wagon and trail rides, and his son Joshua had ringside seats.

"We'd heard people say that a bear was visible from the chair, so we rode up," says Weaver. "We didn't see anything, so we rode back down and saw Dave Wedum [a retired game warden] firing explosive rounds [to haze the bear away from the area]. For some reason, the Glacier Chaser stopped. The grizzly ran right underneath our chair! He obviously knew where he was going. He hopped into the pond, and just like you see on television, he turned onto his back and paddled around!"

"He was a real nice looking griz," says Jeff Gerber, a cat-driver by winter and hill maintenance worker by summer. "I was fixing the pond liner one day, and he came to visit. He was eating tadpoles in the pond, and that's how the plastic liner got torn up."

While bear sightings are fairly unusual, information about bears and other critters in the region is on permanent display in the Summit House at the Environmental Education Center. The cooperative effort between The Big Mountain and the U.S. Forest Service offers visitors a chance to feel the fur of several animals, peek into birds' nests and learn about footprints of different animals, as well as participate in several other interactive exhibits.

The Forest Service marks and maintains the Danny On Trail to the top of The Big Mountain from the Village area, while The Big Mountain maintains the summer "walking museum" around the Village. Some of the original lift apparatus from the Hell-Roaring Ski Club's rope tow, the Sun Valley Mogul Planer grooming device, and an original T-bar's summer passenger chair are on display. Concerts and summer theater take to the stage. Cyclists challenge themselves on mountain bike trails.

Summer Boy Scouts hiking up The Big Mountain.

While the Hell-Roaring Ski Club members might not recognize the Village area, they would welcome the brush-cleared slopes and open expanses to perfect their turns. The miners and the sheep may be gone forever from the slopes, but the bears, the berries and the adventures remain.

License plate on the Alpinglow Inn's truck.

7

A "Spirit of Adventure and Cooperation"

Opposite: Fire on The Big Mountain! The Ski Lodge burned October 31, 1963, just three weeks before the opening of ski season.

"I didn't see Dad for three months while he rebuilt the Ski Lodge then through ski season," says Mary Anne Schenck Miles. "Then he came home and he had gray hair."

Upper right: "The Wet Look" by Jeanne and Gary Tallman, circa 1970.

 If the 1960s brought social confusion to America, the '70s brought fashion confusion to the ski world. After the slim, trim Bogners of the 1950s, the French Olympic team introduced the wet-look, the slicker-than-the-old-Bierstube-floor fabric that allowed a downed skier to slide at Toni Matt speeds into the parking lot. Then flannel shirts and blue jeans, "Montana Bogners," recalls Frank Morrison, became *haute couture*.

Head 360s were pushed off ski racks and replaced by Hart Javelins fiberglass and metal skis. Then Rossignol's Roc 550s flashed red, white and blue across the slopes like flags on the High-line in a stiff breeze.

Although stockholders had not yet seen a return on their investment, The Big Mountain grew. Improvements and additions to the Lodge, the Chalet, the parking lot and lift facilities propelled the ski area into the national press. Then on October 31, 1963, fire severely damaged the Ski Lodge. The *Whitefish Pilot* reported that firemen managed to save part of the building, yet damage costs reached $100,000. Ed Schenck's crew rebuilt the Lodge in a remarkable 45 days.

"For three years after that fire, part of the job of the bartender was changing flat tires," says Corporate Administrator Sandi Hale Unger, employed full time at The Big Mountain since 1962. "To rebuild the Lodge, they bulldozed the charred structure across the parking lot. There were lots of nails left in the parking lot. Finally, we hired the Boy Scouts to pick up the nails."

By 1966, the Great Northern Railway and WSI produced *The Big Mountain of Fun*, a 22-minute 16 millimeter film advertising "wide open runs down a vast mountain." It was the first of several films about The Big Mountain's skiing, including four films by Jim Rice: *Rocky's Big Mountain, Mountain Standard Time, I am the Mountain*, and the critically acclaimed *Cool Winter*. Popular at the regional ski shows, these films were just a part of the burgeoning ski advertising and marketing business that would take representatives from the mountain to ski shows from Vancouver, British Columbia to Miami, Florida. Marion Lacy's photography graced many brochures and advertisements.

"God bless Marion Lacy," says Norm Kurtz. "I don't remember what he ever charged for his photos, but we sure made good time with them."

Early advertising combined Lacy's photos with drawings and maps penned by the ever-talented Ed Schenck or his brother, Aaron. A grinning, skiing mountain goat became the emblem of the mountain, followed by the ptarmigan, then again a mountain goat.

Above: Filmmaker Jim Rice and son, Jim, 1967. Jim filmed and produced four movies of The Big Mountain and several films on other subjects.
Below: Advertisement from 1952 issue of the MONTANA TREASURE *magazine.*

Meanwhile, WSI embarked on a first for Montana: the Alpinglow Inn condominium hotel. Opening the spring of 1969, Alpinglow Inn's 54 units sold for under $10,000 each. Uniquely constructed, the Alpinglow Inn balanced on stilts against the hillside, a design that made doubters suggest that "it would collapse in the first earthquake," says Norm Kurtz, who handled Alpinglow details for WSI. "Later when we had a tremor, the building just sat there and wiggled her hips with no damage."

In 1975 and again in '78, the mountain added new lifts, first replacing the Poma with Chair Three, then adding easier access into the Faults, Langley Run, the North Bowl (Moe-Mentum) and undiscovered points in between with Chair Four. By 1975, The Big Mountain saw 117,000 annual skier visits. Between building the Alpinsnack, adding the Lower Terminal Bar to the Lodge, and affixing night lights above Chair Three slopes, the mountain doubled dining capacity and set pace for more development.

Despite naysayers who forecast that The Big Mountain stock would never pay off, stockholders saw a return on their investment in 1976. According to Sandi Unger, preferred stockholders received dividends in August that year, followed a year later by dividends for common stock. At its 50th anniversary, WSI has over 800 stockholders, and its stock is traded on NASDAQ Small Cap.

"I remember Ed Schenck walking into the board of directors' meeting and telling us we passed the million-dollar mark," says Roy Duff, who served on the board for 28 years. "It was a struggle for the first 20 years."

Other businesses sought outlets on The Big Mountain. In 1977, Jeff Fisher built his Anapurna lodge, followed by Kandahar Lodge in 1981, run by Buck and Mary Pat Love. WSI kept up the pace by building an addition to the Alpinsnack and a new Ski Hut at the base of Chair Four in 1978. Hibernation House was constructed in 1979.

By the time Tim Hinderman took over as general manager of operations in 1983, ski fashions and skier visits brightened. Day-glow colors trimmed ski outfits on the steadily increasing numbers of Big Mountain skiers. Train groups from the Midwest and the Pacific Northwest gave way to bus groups from Canada. By 1985, a new T-bar and more night lights brightened skiing on the Hellroaring slope for the 227,400 annual skier visits. Travelers from Alberta and Saskatchewan represented about 40 percent of winter visitors.

Upon the spot where the early Hell-Roaring skiers once played, the summer

PATCHES COURTESY SANDI UNGER

Canadian racers wearing patches which read 'F-I-S World Ski Championships 1950.'

O Canada!

Canadian visitors to The Big Mountain have long influenced the business of skiing from tickets to real estate. Up to 40 percent of winter visitors come from Alberta and Saskatchewan. Businesses often lure Canadians with "at par" prices. Busy Saturdays have found up to four dozen buses from Canada in The Big Mountain parking lot.

"People just want to get away," says Dawn Hicock of Calgary. "Whitefish is a mini vacation with good skiing and a different atmosphere."

"We come for the skiing and stay for the fun," admits another Albertan. "And some of us just come to ski Mahogany Ridge — you know the run. It's in the Bierstube!"

crews cleared and widened the Ranger Trail to accommodate grooming.

"Over the last decade of skiing, it has become evident that groomed slopes and satisfied skiers go hand in hand," reads a Big Mountain press release dated September 6, 1983. "For this reason, The Big Mountain has added another Kässbohrer Pisten Bully to the grooming fleet."

Skier service topped agendas for the staff. Cushions softened wood seats on some lifts, and tissue boxes adorned the lift corrals.

Perhaps Ed Schenck's greatest unrealized dream before his death in 1982 was the construction of the Summit House, which was completed in 1985. A 1989 addition brought the building's size to 15,700 square feet. To transport cement and construction materials to the 7,000-foot perch, truck drivers drove four or five hours from the valley up a gravel route called Taylor Creek Road to the summit, recalls Bob Yeager, the Facilities Maintenance Supervisor.

"One trucker was fuming because no one told him exactly where he was taking his load," laughs Yeager. "He told us he'd jack-knifed his semi on our road. There were no turnarounds."

And The Big Mountain has hit no turnarounds. From the initial $80,000 investment, WSI's fixed assets grew to $15 million in the 1990s. Nearly 300,000 skiers annually snowplow and schuss The Big Mountain. WSI began selling real estate in 1982 through The Big Mountain Development Corporation. By the mid 1990s, lots that might have sold for a few thousand dollars in the 1950s sold for $70,000 to $190,000. The Big Mountain claims less than two dozen full-time residents, yet over 71 homesites encompass the four current phases of Sunrise Ridge development. Homeowners, businesses and WSI formed the Big Mountain Resort Association in 1993 to benefit the mountain community, provide a forum for problem solving, and generate funds for a community facility.

While the improvements of the mountain's second 25 years brought more and more skiers to the northern outpost, the "friendly service" advertised in the 1950s did not falter in the minds of guests. Up until the Chalet closed as a lodging facility in 1983, guests who arrived late

Whitefish train station depot reflecting The Big Mountain.

Hank Hibbing finds deep powder skiing New Year's Eve, 1983.

The Empire Builder advertising photo shoot by Marion Lacy with Jeanne Tallman, Marian Livers, Leo Fisher, Roy Duff (holding skis) Jake Heckathorn and Dick Collins, circa 1960.

Another First on The Big Mountain

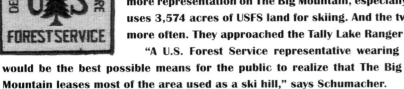

When Bob Schumacher retired from a career with the Montana Department of Fish and Game as a fisheries biologist, he planned to ski every day. In 1982, he and his friend Howard Whitney, a retired U.S. Customs and Immigrations border patrolman, decided that perhaps the U.S. Forest Service needed more representation on The Big Mountain, especially since The Big Mountain uses 3,574 acres of USFS land for skiing. And the two retirees needed to ski more often. They approached the Tally Lake Ranger with a suggestion.

"A U.S. Forest Service representative wearing a recognizable uniform would be the best possible means for the public to realize that The Big Mountain leases most of the area used as a ski hill," says Schumacher. "As a senior citizen, the midweek pass price was not prohibitive. Maybe I needed an excuse to go skiing."

They arranged the Ski Host program that has since been copied by other ski areas in the West.

"During the second year of the Ski Host program, the Forest Service had a workshop on the mountain for snow rangers from about 15 National Forests in the West," he says. "Howard and I were asked to put in an appearance and make a few comments on our program. Many of the programs on the other forests started after that workshop."

During the years since they initiated the Ski Host program, four other volunteers joined their ranks. They assist the snow ranger in taking measurements for water content of snow; they ski all the runs and talk to skiers who seem puzzled about trail direction; they gather The Big Mountain's surveys from the public.

"I'm just doing what I did before I had the green jacket on," laughs Ski Host Jessie Harring. "I talk, talk, talk to people — on the chair, in the Summit House and on the slopes."

US Forest Service Ski Hosts Jessie Harring and Bob Schumacher. Schumacher and Howard Whitney began the program in 1982.

Dashing Through the Snow

"On New Year's Eve in 1982, a night colder than hell, Steve Greibrook ran sleigh rides," recalls Jeff Fisher, who contracted the rides for his Anapurna guests and others. "It was late, and Steve came in our little store to turn in money, warm up, then return the horses to the barn."

The cowboy had tied the reins to the bumper of a Volkswagen.

"The horses pulled back a bit on the reins and since the Volkswagen was parked on ice, it slipped back," said Fisher, who noted that the moving vehicle did little to add confidence to the nervous equine. "The reins broke, and the horses went racing toward the barn, around the corner past Kandahar into the parking lot, full blast. They ran headstrong into the back of my Bronco pickup, which I'd let Steve use earlier to drive out to the barn. When we got there, one horse lay under the Bronco which had all four wheels off ground. The sleigh sat in the box of the Bronco."

Fisher says they patched up the Bronco and "drove it as a junker for a while."

And what of the horses? "Oh, they just came out with a few scratches."

found a friendly letter, recalls ski instructor Hoagy Carmichael.

"If guests came in late, they'd find a note saying, 'Hi, here's your room key. If you're hungry, the kitchen is open,'" says Carmichael.

Large ski groups arriving by train are still met by The Big Mountain's staff, as advertised in a 1947 brochure. Ski school still offers a weekly Fall-Line Hour, now called Powder Hour, and ski patrol still hosts the weekly Frabert Awards.

What's to come in the next 50 years in a maturing industry will be directed by a number of factors as uncontrollable as weather and the economy, to marketing strategies and snowboarding and skiing popularity.

"The assets of The Big Mountain today are the same as they were 50 years ago: a great mountain, great people, and that terrific 'Montana atmosphere,'" says Chief Executive Officer Michael Collins. "Looking to the future, we will continue to grow, both the mountain and our unique village. Our challenge will be to continue delivering an outstanding resort experience for all our guests, while at the same time maintaining our Big Mountain assets that make us so special."

Torchlight parade down the face of Chair Two, 1985.

Top right: Winter Carnival, February 1962, at Queen's Coronation Banquet. Russell Street, Mary Jane Street, Art La Brie (King Ullr 11th of 1961), Susan Monroe (Abell), Queen 1962, and Dick Adams, Prime Minister 1961.

Yetis for Winter Carnival

Ullr patch
COURTESY SANDI UNGER

Kathy Sullivan, owner of Mountain Photography, poses on the other side of the lens in powder. Sullivan and her dog, Humphrey, entertained guests for years during Fall-Line Hour.

Meteorologically Challenged

Mother Nature has always blessed The Big Mountain with abundant snowfall. Even during dry years in most of the West, The Big Mountain records sizable snowpacks. The average snowfall is over 300 inches annually.

What skiers want to know, however, are the current conditions. In the 1950s, Ed Schenck gave daily ski reports, and newspapers as far away as Spokane published daily reports, but it wasn't until the 1960s that mountain personalities added humor and pizazz to the snow reports. Skiers wanted to know four basics: wind speed, new snow, visibility, and temperature. And under no circumstances were the snow reporters to use the word FOG!

"That presented a problem once in a while," says reformed snow reporter John Porterfield, a.k.a. "Johnny Powderfield," whose voice blessed the radio reports for seven years. "We had to get a bit creative in describing the conditions on the mountain. We had to be honest, yet we often gave the reports a funny twist."

Norm Kurtz, who coined the phrase, "Skiing in Montana is about as much fun as you can have with your clothes on," assured skiers that the "occluded visibility" included "low clouds."

"That's not fog up there," Gary Elliott of Bierstube fame tells customers who come in and drip their sorrows all over the Stube floor. "That's slow light, I tell them. One time I was driving up the mountain on a particularly nasty day," recalls Elliott, "and I tuned into Norm Kurtz's snow report. Now it was snowing and blowing and the visibility was probably about ten inches. Norm gets on the radio and gives the conditions on Chair Two and Chair Three, and the Village area. Toward the end, he says, 'As far as the conditions are on Chair One, we assume that everything's okay because we send the chairs up and they keep coming back!' I laughed until I cried."

Although The Big Mountain is not known for wind, once in a while a breeze charges across the region.

"One day it was so windy that the Chalet was actually shaking," recalls Porterfield. "The Chalet shook so bad that there were whitecaps in the toilets!"

In 1985, when snow didn't appear until Christmas, even Kurtz was ready to make deals with devils. Norm had affixed a sign near a big box on the side of the Chalet that read "Norm's Snow Switch."

He said, "If it snows a foot, I'll give up redheads. If it snows two feet, I'll give up ketchup."

At last report he still uses ketchup.

Left to right: Brochure from 1951-52 ski season; Ski The Big Mountain brochure from 1961; Ski Big brochure from 1966; and brochure from the days when tickets were $21, 1988-89.

Summit House, Glacier view.

And about that "friendly service"? Says mountain resident Peter Brucato, "Just look at the view from here. I watch the sun rise over Columbia Mountain every morning, and the sun set over Chair Three every evening. This is a beautiful place we live in, Montana. Sometimes we lose sight of that beauty while we struggle with every day challenges. When I look out on this sun setting, I think about all the wonderful people I've met here on The Big Mountain. That's what's truly important in life. Friends."

Although Schenck struggled financially for most of the 35 years he put into the ski business, he was proud of his accomplishments. Schenck told the *Saturday Evening Post* in 1950, "[T]here are few people in town who don't feel personally proud of Big Mountain. You can see it from almost anywhere in town. It stands out from the other mountains to the north because of the wide, crisscrossed patterns, like an enormous figure four, that the ski runs etch in its evergreen cover. Somehow, [The Big Mountain] has become a concrete expression of the town's spirit of adventure and cooperation."

JEAN ARTHUR

About the Author

Jean Arthur writes and photographs from her Whitefish, Montana home. Her first nationally published magazine article about skiing appeared in a 1983 issue of *Skiing Magazine*. The topic: The Big Mountain. Since then, numerous regional, national and international publications have showcased her writing and photography including *Smithsonian*, *American Heritage*, *Adventure West* and *Montana Magazine*.

Born in Portland, Oregon in 1960, Arthur pursued writing as a youngster, covering high school events for a local newspaper. Her first grade teacher noted in Arthur's first report card that, "Jean will be a writer someday!" She received a Bachelor of Arts degree from the University of Oregon Journalism School, and a Master of Fine Arts degree from the University of Montana Creative Writing program.

In Montana since 1980, Arthur and her husband, Lynn Sellegren, traipse through the mountains with their children, Eric, Gretchen and Bridger.

MARION LACY

About the Primary Photographer

Marion Lacy above all loved the mountains. He photographed skiing and scenery for nearly a half century, often carrying 40 pounds of camera gear into the back country or to the top of the Hell-Roaring Ski Slope.

"He was very supportive of The Big Mountain," recalls his daughter, Sheila Lacy Morrison. "He took a lot of photos to help Ed Schenck out, and did that specifically as a personal, a civic thing."

Born Marion Elwood Lacy in Oklahoma in 1910, he learned the art of photography as a youngster in his father's Hoopston, Illinois photography studio. He moved west after high school, and for a time operated a studio in Walla Walla, Washington before opening Lacy's Photo Studio in Whitefish in 1944. He made portraits of people, mountains and wildlife until he sold the studio in 1976.

Lacy received several prestigious awards and national recognition for his Glacier National Park scenics, and in 1970 was inducted into the Honorary Society of Photography. Called the Ansel Adams of Montana, Lacy died in 1980.

"The mountains have a very private feeling," Lacy once said. "They are open; they mean freedom; they provide escape."

Writer's Notes

The bulk of the research for *Hellroaring: 50 Years on The Big Mountain* resulted from primary research through personal interviews during 1995 and '96. Other research materials are listed below. I'd like to thank the people who not only contributed information to the research process, but who saved memorabilia and donated items to the Stumptown Historical Society. I found the following sources helpful in creating this book: The best general study for details on a half-century of skiing The Big Mountain can be found in the Flathead County Library's collections of *The Whitefish Pilot*, 1947-96, and *The Hungry Horse News*, 1947-96. Ed Schenck's story as told to Edmund Christopherson, "They Bet Their Shirts on Skiing" can be found in the March 4, 1950, issue of *The Saturday Evening Post*. Rick Graetz wrote an overview of the mountain's fortieth anniversary, published in *Montana Magazine*, December, 1987. The Montana Historical Society in Helena has a few holdings regarding skiing and The Big Mountain. Hidden in the eaves of The Big Mountain's Chalet are the bulk of archival photographs by Marion Lacy.